THE
AYN RAND
COLUMN

THE
AYN RAND
COLUMN

Written for the *Los Angeles Times*

Edited with an Introduction
by Peter Schwartz

Second Renaissance Books
New Milford, Connecticut

Published by Second Renaissance Books
143 West Street, New Milford, CT 06776
www.rationalmind.com

First Printing, November, 1991
Revised Second Edition, October, 1998
10 9 8 7 6 5 4 3 2 1

Copyright © 1971, 1976, 1977, 1978, 1979 by Ayn Rand
Copyright © 1998 by the Estate of Ayn Rand
Introduction Copyright © 1998 by Peter Schwartz

Library of Congress Cataloging-in-Publication Data

Rand, Ayn.
      [Selections. 1998]
      The Ayn Rand column : written for the Los Angeles times / edited
with an introduction by Peter Schwartz.—Rev. 2nd ed.
p. cm.
Includes index.
ISBN 1-56114-292-1
I. Schwartz, Peter. II. Los Angeles times. III. Title
PS3535.A547A6   1998
814' .52—dc21   98-7897
                                                                              CIP

Designed by M.J. Trollope
Printed in the United States of America

PUBLISHER'S NOTE TO THE SECOND EDITION:

Ayn Rand's place in history has been assured by her brilliant skills as novelist and as philosopher. Her intellectual influence is becoming ever more evident. Her books sell some 300,000 copies annually worldwide, while her previously unpublished writings and ideas are now being made available through the posthumous release of her letters, journals and taped seminars. Ayn Rand (and her philosophy of Objectivism) is a growing source of films, articles and philosophical discussion—over 15 years after her death.

The Ayn Rand Column (first published in 1991) is one more work in that series. In it she brings her talent to analyzing the news and cultural events of the time in a weekly newspaper column written for the *Los Angles Times* during 1962.

This expanded edition includes three out-of-print and unanthologized essays. "Textbook of Americanism" (1946) originally appeared in *The Vigil*, a publication of The Motion Picture Alliance for the Preservation of American Ideals. The first third of an uncompleted project, its purpose was to define and clarify the basic principles involved in political issues. The second essay, "The Fascist New Frontier" (1962), addresses the moral-political philosophy dominating modern culture. (Two of the newspaper columns from *The Ayn Rand Column,* "An Intellectual Coup d'État" and "Government by Intimidation," are excerpted in part from this extensive discussion.) The final article is her contribution to a 1958 symposium on the individualism-vs-collectivism choice faced by business managers, particularly those influenced by the book *The Organization Man.*

June 1998

CONTENTS

INTRODUCTION

One of Ayn Rand's distinctive virtues is her ability to examine what outwardly appears to be the most ordinary, trivial, sterile event—and to draw the most fascinating implications from it. This talent is not primarily a result of her writing skills, impressive as they are; it is the consequence of certain *thinking* skills. Her cognitive approach is always to think in essentials—to brush aside the minutiae surrounding some concrete event, to identify the fundamentals, to extract the underlying principle. This is what enables her to draw the widest conclusions from the narrowest facts. And this is why her comments on current events remain so illuminating decades later, even after one's memory of the specifics may have faded. Principles, by their nature, are of timeless concern.

The essays in *The Ayn Rand Column* bear testimony to this.

Ayn Rand wrote most of them in her role as columnist for the *Los Angeles Times* in 1962. They deal with the events described in the newspaper headlines of the time. Yet, unlike so much other journalistic commentary—which is stale and irrelevant just days, or hours, after it is written—virtually nothing of hers becomes outdated. Her perspective on the news is not that of the daily reporter, but that of the grand historian whose time frame is the centuries and whose function is to explain the world by reference to universal truths. Whether she is scrutinizing Algeria's civil war or England's entry into the Common Market or Alger Hiss' appearance on television—Ayn Rand always has something of enduring interest to communicate. She looks at the Algerian conflict, for example, and shows how "a majority without an ideology is a helpless mob, to be taken over by anyone"; or at the controversy over the Common Market and reveals why, to the liberals, "international democracy, a World Government and an unlimited majority rule are ideals only so long as the majority votes for socialism;" or at the protests and counter-protests over ABC's interview of the Soviet agent Hiss and explains that freedom of speech "does not demand that private citizens provide a microphone for the man who advocates their destruction."

Her characteristic method of seeking out the non-obvious is equally evident in the supplementary articles in this collection. It is, for example, uniquely Ayn Rand—an intransigent atheist and egoist—who could write a piece defending the secular value of Christmas gift-giving. It is uniquely Ayn Rand who could explore what at first glance is a prosaic, parochial subject—the hobby of stamp collecting—and conclude that the activity appeals particularly to the psycho-epistemology of the productive mind because it "has the essential elements of a career, but transposed to a clearly delimited, intensely private world." To Ayn Rand, a first glance was never a final one.

* * * *

I am very pleased that Second Renaissance Books—of which I am president and which carries the most extensive selection of Ayn Rand's writings available—is inaugurating its entry into the book publishing field with *The Ayn Rand Column*. And I would like to thank Walter Huebscher, Don Lemont, Catherine Dickerson and Edward Podritske for their work in producing this book.

While some of the essays in this anthology have been reprinted elsewhere (primarily in *The Objectivist Newsletter*), the majority will come as new reading even for most of Ayn Rand's fans. I hope you find the book enlightening, and that you look forward to future titles to be published by Second Renaissance Books.

Peter Schwartz
September 1991

<u>Summaries:</u>

June 17 "<u>Introducing Objectivism</u>" (Summary of Objectivism — altruism as destroyer of capitalism — examples)
(Ethics - politics)

June 24 "<u>War and Peace</u>" (Against statist peace-movements — altruism as source of war, capitalism - of peace
(Politics - capitalism & war)

July 1 "<u>Progress or Sacrifice</u>" ("Economic growth" vs "Social gains")
(Politics & - economics)

July 8 "<u>The New Enemies of 'The Untouchables'</u>" — (Value-disintegration in art — romanticism — matter of TV censorship)
(Art & - culture)

July 15 "<u>An Intellectual Coup d'État</u>" (Analysis of Kennedy's Yale speech + its obvious statism)
(Politics - theory)

July 22 "<u>The Cold Civil War</u>" (The 'civil war' of a "mixed economy" — illustrated by: NAM - Labor "Medicare" - the Press)
(Politics - illustrated theory)

July 29 "<u>Government by Intimidation</u>" (Celler's proposed antitrust inquiry on press)
(Politics - press & antitrust)

August 5 — "_Let Us Alone!_" (The origin of the term "_Laissez-faire_"
(Politics ½ ⁻) (history + theory))

August 12 — "_Just Suppose_" (Advice to the Republicans on tax-
exemptions for education) (Politics ½ -
taxes + education.)

August 19 — "_Through Your Most Grievous Fault_"
(The death of Marilyn
Monroe) (Art – Culture)

August 26 — "_An Open Letter To My Readers_" (Acknowledgment — "The public
does this " – The Authorized Sources on
Objectivism – the answer to attackers)
(Personal – Culture)

September 2 — "_Mickey Spillane_" (His value + the reason of the attacks
on him – review of "The Girl Hunters",
(Art – Culture)

September 9 — "_The Dying Victim of Berlin_" (Foreign policy : Kennedy +
Brazilian students – the meaning of
the East Berlin atrocities.)
(Politics – foreign policy)

September 16 — "_Ninety-Three_" (A review of Hugo's "Ninety-Three" –
Hugo as the antidote to today's
cult of depravity.)
(Art – Culture)

The
Ayn Rand
Column

Introducing Objectivism

JUNE 17, 1962—At a sales conference at Random House, preceding the publication of *Atlas Shrugged*, one of the book salesmen asked me whether I could present the essence of my philosphy while standing on one foot. I did, as follows:

1. *Metaphysics*:   Objective Reality
2. *Epistemology*:   Reason
3. *Ethics*:   Self-interest
4. *Politics*:   Capitalism

If you want this translated into simple language, it would read: 1. "Nature, to be commanded, must be obeyed" or "Wishing won't make it so." 2. "You can't eat your cake and have it, too." 3. "Man is an end in himself." 4. "Give me liberty or give me death."

If you held these concepts with total consistency, as the base of your convictions, you would have a full philosophical system to guide the course of your life. But to hold them with total consistency—to understand, to define, to prove and to apply them—requires volumes of thought. Which is why philosophy cannot be discussed while standing on one foot—nor while standing on two feet on both sides of every fence. This last is the predominant philosophical position today, particularly in the field of politics.

In the space of a column, I can give only the briefest summary of my position, as a frame-of-reference for all my future columns. My philosophy, Objectivism, holds that:

1. Reality exists as an objective absolute—facts are facts, independent of man's feelings, wishes, hopes or fears.

2. Reason (the faculty which identifies and integrates the material provided by man's senses) is man's only means of perceiving reality, his only source of knowledge, his only guide to action, and his basic means of survival.

3. Man—every man—is an end in himself, not the means to the ends of others. He must exist for his own sake, neither sacrificing himself to others nor sacrificing others to himself. The pursuit of his own *rational* self-interest and of his own happiness is the highest moral

purpose of his life.

4. The ideal political-economic system is laissez-faire capitalism. It is a system where men deal with one another, not as victims and executioners, nor as masters and slaves, but as *traders*, by free, voluntary exchange to mutual benefit. It is a system where no man may obtain any values from others by resorting to physical force, and *no man may initiate the use of physical force against others.* The government acts only as a policeman that protects man's rights; it uses physical force *only* in retaliation and *only* against those who initiate its use, such as criminals or foreign invaders. In a system of full capitalism, there should be (but, historically, has not yet been) a complete separation of state and economics, in the same way and for the same reasons as the separation of state and church.

Capitalism was the system originated in the United States. Its success, its progress, its achievements are unprecedented in human history. America's political philosophy was based on man's right to his own life, to his own liberty, to the pursuit of his own happiness, which means: on man's right to exist for his own sake. That was America's *implicit* moral code, but it had not been formulated explicitly. This was the flaw in her intellectual armor, which is now destroying her. America and capitalism are perishing for lack of a moral base.

The destroyer is the morality of altruism.

Altruism holds that man has no right to exist for his own sake, that service to others is the only moral justification of his existence, and that self-sacrifice is his highest moral duty. The political expression of altruism is collectivism or *statism*, which holds that man's life and work belong to the state—to the society, to the group, the gang, the race, the nation—and that the state may dispose of him in any way it pleases for the sake of whatever it deems to be its own tribal, collective good.

"From her start, America was torn by the clash of her political system with the altruist morality. Capitalism and altruism are incompatible; they cannot coexist in the same man or in the same society. Today, the conflict has reached its ultimate climax; the choice is clearcut: either a new morality of rational self-interest, with its consequences of freedom, justice, progress and man's happiness on earth—or the primordial morality of altruism, with its consequences of slavery, brute force, stagnant terror and sacrificial furnaces." (*For the New Intellectual*)

You may observe the practical results of altruism and statism all around us in today's world—such as the slave-labor camps of Soviet Russia, where twenty-one million political prisoners work on the construction of government projects and die of *planned* malnutrition, human life being cheaper than food—or the gas chambers and mass slaughter of Nazi Germany—or the terror and starvation of Red China—or the hysteria of Cuba where the government offers men for sale—or the wall of East Berlin where human beings leap from roofs or crawl through sewers in order to escape, while guards shoot at fleeing *children*.

Observe these atrocities, then ask yourself whether any of it would be possible if men had not accepted the idea that man is a sacrificial animal to be immolated for the sake of the "public good." Read the speeches of those countries' political leaders and ask yourself what arguments would be left to them if the word "sacrifice" were regarded not as a moral ideal, but as the anti-human evil which it is.

And *then*, listen to the speeches of our present Administration—and ask yourself the same question.

War and Peace

JUNE 24, 1962—One of the ugliest characteristics of today's world is the mixture of frantic war preparations with hysterical peace propaganda, and the fact that *both come from the same source*—from the same political philosophy. If mankind is ever to achieve peace, the first step will be made when people realize that today's peace movements are *not* advocates of peace.

Professing love and concern for the survival of mankind, these movements keep screaming that nuclear weapons have made war too horrible to contemplate, that armed force and violence should be abolished as a means of settling disputes among nations, and that war should be outlawed in the name of humanity. Yet these same peace movements do not oppose dictatorships; the political views of their members range through all shades of the statist spectrum, from "welfare statism" to socialism to communism. This means that these movements are opposed to the use of coercion by one nation against another, but not by the government of a nation against its own citizens; it means that they are opposed to the use of force and violence against *armed* adversaries but not against the *disarmed*.

Under any political system, in any organized society, the government holds a legal monopoly on the use of physical force. *That* is the crucial difference between a government and any private organization. Private individuals or groups deal with one another peacefully, by means of trade, persuasion, discussion and voluntary agreements; they cannot resort to force; those who do, are criminals—and it is the proper duty of the government to restrain them.

In a free, civilized society, the use of physical force is outlawed by the recognition of man's inalienable, individual rights. The power of the government is limited by law to the role of a policeman that protects men's rights and uses force only against those who initiate its use. *This* is the basic political principle of the only social system that banishes force from human relationships: laissez-faire capitalism.

But a statist system—whether of a communist, fascist, Nazi, socialist or "welfare" type—is based on the opposite principle: on the government's unlimited power, which means: on the rule of brute force. The differences among statist systems are only a matter of time and degree; the principle is the same. Under statism, the government is not a policemen, but a legalized criminal that holds the power to use physical force in any manner and for any purpose it pleases against legally disarmed, defenseless victims.

Nothing can ever justify so monstrously evil a theory. Nothing can justify the horror, the brutality, the plunder, the destruction, the starvation, the slave-labor camps, the torture chambers, the wholesale slaughter of statist dictatorships. Yet *this* is what today's alleged peace-lovers are willing to advocate or tolerate—in the name of love for humanity.

Statism is a system of institutionalized violence and perpetual civil war, that leaves men no choice but to fight to seize power over one another. In a full dictatorship, that civil war takes the form of bloody purges, as in Nazi Germany and Soviet Russia. In a "mixed economy," it takes the form of "pressure group" warfare, each group fighting for legislation to extort its own advantages by *force* from all other groups.

Statism is nothing more than gang rule. A statist dictatorship is a gang devoted to looting the effort of the productive citizens of its own country. When statist rulers exhaust their own country's economy and run out of loot, they attack their neighbors. All the major wars of history were started by the more controlled economies of the time against the freer ones. For instance, World War I was started by monarchist Germany and Czarist Russia, which were "mixed economies" of a predominantly statist kind. World War II was started by the alliance of Nazi Germany with Soviet Russia and their joint attack on Poland.

Observe that in World War II, Germany and Russia dismantled entire factories in conquered countries, to ship them home—while the freest one of the "mixed economies," the semi-capitalistic United States, sent billions worth of lend-lease equipment, including entire factories, to its allies. Germany and Russia needed war; the United States did not and gained nothing. Yet it is capitalism that today's peace-lovers oppose and statism that they advocate—in the name of peace.

There is no moral justification for the vicious doctrine that some men have the right to rule others by force. But so long as men continue to believe that some sort of alleged "noble purpose" can justify it—violence, bloodshed and wars will continue.

It is true that nuclear weapons have made wars too horrible to contemplate. But it makes no difference to a man whether he is killed by a nuclear bomb or is led to a Nazi gas chamber or a Soviet firing squad, with no voices raised to defend him. Will such a man feel any love or concern for the survival of mankind? Or will he be more justified in feeling that a cannibalistic mankind, which tolerates dictatorships, does not deserve to survive?

Let those who are seriously concerned with peace, those who do love *man* and do care about his survival, realize that war cannot be outlawed by lawless statist thugs and that it is not war but *force* that has to be outlawed.

Progress or Sacrifice

JULY 1, 1962—Statists may ride to power by dispensing promises, threats and handouts to the seekers of the unearned—but they find themselves impotent in a national emergency, because the language, methods and policies which were successful with parasites do not work when the country needs producers.

The present behavior of the Kennedy Administration can serve as an eloquent example.

The Administration's policy rests on two proclaimed goals or slogans which represent an irreconcilable contradiction: "social gains" and "economic growth."

"Social gains," as the term is used today, does not mean the economic progress earned by a particular group in free trade on a free market, but the unearned advantages or handouts granted to it by the government, which means: extorted by legalized force from the productive effort of other groups.

"Economic growth" means the rise of an economy's productivity, due to the discovery of new knowledge, new products, new techniques, which means: due to the achievements of men's productive ability.

The seekers of "social gains" exist in every economic class, group or profession—and their political philosophy is welfare statism. It divorces achievement from rewards, or production from distribution, and redistributes a country's wealth, penalizing the more productive in favor of the less productive. No matter how mixed a "mixed economy" becomes—forcing every social class to prey on every other—its real warfare is not *between* social classes, but *within* them. The power of welfare statism rests on special pressure groups who prey on the abler members of their own class by means of an enforced, unearned economic equality.

Franklin D. Roosevelt came to power declaring that the problem of production had been solved once and for all, and that our only problem was that of distribution. But after thirty years of "redistributing," the Kennedy Administration has come up against the fact that production is not an automatic gift of nature and that it depends on certain conditions, which no welfare-state economist dares consider.

9

During those thirty years, the productive elements of our economy—the creators of "economic growth"—have been throttled, shackled, paralyzed and all but destroyed. Seniority rules or automatic, collective promotions have almost eliminated the ablest workers' chance to rise, holding them down to the productive level of the less competent. Grotesque antitrust prosecutions have beaten down the best industrial concerns, penalizing them for productive success, in favor of any unsuccessful competitor. (And while such companies as General Electric, General Motors, United States Steel are being constantly dragged into antitrust courts—while business executives are being sent to jail—men with political pull, like Billie Sol Estes, are making fortunes.) The productive arteries of America were split open by the progressive income tax, and the handouts of "social gains" spurted across national boundaries, oozing, like blood, to the darkest corners of the globe's jungles.

Who can pay for it all? "Our economic growth," cries Mr. Kennedy—while seeking frantically to create new pressure groups to buttress his power, such as a youth group (the "Peace Corps"), an age group ("Medicare"), a "consumers" group (courted in a long speech on the alleged "rights" of consumers, with not a word about the rights of the forgotten men: the producers).

It is Mr. Kennedy's attempt to treat the producers as if they, too, were a special pressure group seeking the unearned, that exposes the bankruptcy of the welfare state. As an incentive to "economic growth," Mr. Kennedy offered businessmen two "social gains": (a) the tariff bill, which would give him discretionary power to raise or lower tariffs, thus leaving the fate of countless industries at the mercy of his unpredictable favor—and (b) the tax reform bill, which would permit businessmen to keep some part of their own money, with strings attached in the form of tax allowance for expanded capacity.

Mr. Kennedy declared himself to be hurt, disappointed and bewildered by the fact that businessmen did not respond enthusiastically to these favors. The welfare-state philosophy seems to be so axiomatic in his mind that he acted as if he actually believed that the government owns the total income, property and resources of the United States—and that a permission to keep some of the money one has earned should be gratefully regarded as a handout.

Mr. Kennedy seems to have lost the concept of the difference between the goals, the requirements and the psychology of parasites and of producers.

Parasites seek to be taken care of, but producers seek the responsibility of choice and decision. Parasites do not look beyond the range of the immediate moment, but producers have to see and plan long-range. Parasites rely on the good will and the capricious favor of a benefactor—but producers do not live by favor and cannot function or build gigantic industries which the whim of a ruler may wipe out at any moment. What the producers need is not handouts, but freedom. And freedom is not among the gifts that the welfare state has the power to dispense.

While Mr. Kennedy is pouting about the businessmen's lack of confidence in his "good will," and (substituting brashness for proof) is proclaiming the oldest bromides of statism's mythology, the United States economy is not growing, but running down. (And the stock market plunge of May 28, a grim avenger of the helpless steel industry, was like a heart attack, a warning of what awaits us farther beyond the New Frontier.)

Mr. Kennedy has been constantly invoking both "progress" and "sacrifice." But these two are opposites, and the choice confronting us now is either "progress" or "sacrifice." Either "economic growth" or "social gains." Either freedom or welfare-statist collapse—and our time is running out.

The New Enemies of "The Untouchables"

JULY 8, 1962—When a culture is dominated by an irrational philosophy, a major symptom of its decadence is the inversion of all values. This can always be seen clearly in the field of art, the best barometer of a culture. In today's flood of criticism and abuse, unleashed against the television industry, it is the best program that has been singled out for the most persistent denunciations. That program is "The Untouchables."

The moral meaning and psychological motives of those denunciations are of much deeper significance than the superficiality of the attackers might indicate.

The attacks are spearheaded by the statists inside and outside the F.C.C., who propose to place television and radio under total government control, to establish censorship-by-license-revoking, and to dictate the content of programs by bureaucratic edict, which means: by force. Simultaneously and as a justification for it, they clamor that the television industry is corrupting the public taste by too many shows that feature force and violence.

Crime stories and Westerns are the main target of the statists' attack, in alliance with sundry busybodies of all political denominations, who are always to be found in any pro-censorship movement of the left or the right.

The truth of the matter is the exact opposite of their allegations: the appeal of crime stories and Westerns does not lie in the element of violence, but in the element of moral conflict and moral purpose.

Crime stories and Westerns are the last remnant of romanticism on our airwaves. No matter how primitive their terms, they deal with the most realistic issue of man's life: the battle of good and evil. They present man as a purposeful being who is able to choose his goals, to fight for his values, to resist disaster, to struggle and to win. The best of such stories offer the invaluable elements of a purposeful plot structure, of ingenuity and suspense, of the daring, the unusual, the exciting.

Compare this with what passes for serious drama on today's television screens: slack-faced, loose-lipped characters with unseeing eyes and unfocused minds, who utter self-consciously ungrammatical lines and jerk hysterically through a sprawling mess of pointless happenings, purporting to show man's helplessness or loneliness or essential depravity—all of it adding up to a scream of "I couldn't help it!"—or to a maudlin, mawkish whine of sympathy for some subhuman object who doesn't know why he murders people, he just does—with, occasionally, some stale corn to the effect that life is a rat race.

There are "sophisticated" crime stories, produced by the same modern mentality, which present both the criminals and the detectives as cynical, larcenous, indistinguishable barroom buddies, with brutal fist fights as a substitute for plot—and there are those queer mongrels: the "psychological" Westerns that present a hostility-sublimating sheriff and a cattle rustler with an Oedipus complex. These may indeed appeal to the lowest element of the public's taste. But they come up and perish, unnoticed, every season. It is not by means of fist fights, chases or gun duels that the successful, popular shows hold audiences glued to TV sets year after year.

"The Untouchables" is one of the most successful programs and fully deserves its success. It is a profoundly moral show. In writing, acting and direction, it is a masterpiece of stylized characterization. It captures the essence of the gangster psychology: the irrationality, the hysteria, the chronic terror, the panic. These gangsters are neither glamorized strong-men nor innocent "victims of society"; they are scared rats. They are presented as loathsome, but not frightening, because not powerful; they are presented as contemptible. No child or adult could ever feel inspired to emulate a Frank Nitti.

But Robert Stack's superlative portrayal of Eliot Ness is the most inspiring image on today's screen, the only image of a real hero.

By the austere, unsmiling grimness of his manner, the total self-confidence even in moments of temporary defeat, so total that it can afford to be unstressed, the controlled intensity, the quietly absolute dedication to the moral justice of his task, Stack conveys the integrity of a truly untouchable man—a man whom evil cannot tempt, because it has nothing to offer him. By the faint, occasional hints of a bitterly patient weariness, he projects that fighting evil is not a lark or a glamorous adventure, but a grim job and a deadly battle. And the constantly intense perceptiveness of his attitude—the attitude of a man fully in control and a mind fully in focus—projects the nature of that battle:

man's intellect versus brute force.

Compare "The Untouchables" to the militant mindlessness of today's "serious" dramas and ask yourself which is more likely to give men hope, courage and an hour's refuelling for the battle against the sordid ugliness of today's headlines. And, if moral influence on children is your concern, ask yourself which will help to shape a child's moral character: the conviction that justice, values, struggles and victories are possible, and that there are heroes he can live up to—or the conviction that nothing is possible and anything is permissible, that the good he desperately longs for is an illusion, but the evil that tempts him will bring him loving sympathy, that nobody can help what he does and there is no way out of the incomprehensible terror with which life seems to confront him. Which will shape his soul? Which made you, perhaps, renounce yours?

In view of the virtues of "The Untouchables," what is it that the "touchables" resent and denounce? Precisely its virtues. Not its criminals, but the triumph over criminals. Not the violence, but the moral absolutism.

It is part of today's profound revolt against man, against the intellect, against human efficacy and, above all, against moral values.

An Intellectual Coup d'État

JULY 15,1962—In the 1930s, the advocates of capitalism were warning this country that the welfare state would necessarily lead to growing government controls and ultimately to a totalitarian dictatorship. The liberals denied it vehemently. Today, when these predictions are coming true, when the political principles on which they were based are proved to be right, the liberals' sole answer is that the principles are irrelevant now because these are the 1960s, not the 1930s.

It is significant that Mr. Kennedy chose to deliver a speech, in which this sort of stuff was labeled as "thinking" and "realism," to the students of Yale University. Under its brashly cynical tone, that speech was the frantic plea of a man who knows that he has no valid theory, no rational answers or arguments to offer—and who, therefore, entreats intellectuals to abandon the intellect.

Mr. Kennedy was begging his audience to drop such "illusions" as conceptual knowledge, theories, principles, abstractions, and to consider only the specific problems of our day, singly, never relating one problem to another. This means: to adopt the concrete bound mentality of a Babbitt or a savage who does not look past the range of the immediate moment, sees nothing but immediate problems, and solves them without reference to any principles, usually by means of a club.

No caricature of a Babbitt could project quite so venomous a hatred of the intellect. "Illusions," "truisms," "stereotypes," "myths," "cliches," "platitudes," "slogans," "labels," "incantations," "rhetoric" are the terms Mr. Kennedy used to describe—what? Since he avoided naming it explicitly, one has to read his entire speech to discover the enemy on whom all that abuse was poured. The enemy is philosophy, ideology, principles, ideas—or any man who applies them to political problems.

No, it was not against any particular ideology that that speech was directed, but against ideology as such. It was not businessmen or Republicans or "conservatives" that Mr. Kennedy was denouncing, but all those who raise the obstacle of principles in the path of governmental action.

The example of Western Europe, he asserted, shows that "governments, prepared to face technical problems without ideological pre-

15

conceptions, can coordinate the elements of a national economy to bring about unexampled growth and prosperity."

What causes economic growth? What is the source of prosperity? How does one "coordinate" a national economy? All such questions are irrelevant, according to Mr. Kennedy; a government should act, rule, control, unhampered by any theoretical knowledge; political science and economics are "ideological preconceptions."

As an example of a specific, practical, non-ideological problem, Mr. Kennedy offered the following: "How in sum, can we make our free economy work at full capacity—that is, provide adequate profits for enterprise, adequate wages for labor, adequate utilization of plant and adequate opportunity for all?"

Since all politico-economic principles are to be discarded, by what standard does one determine what is "adequate"? And who determines it? Mr. Kennedy did not say.

"What is at stake in our economic decisions today is, not some grand warfare of rival ideologies, but the practical management of the modern economy," said Mr. Kennedy.

At a time when every country in the world (including the enslaved ones) is torn by the life-and-death struggle of two opposite ideologies—freedom vs. statism—Mr. Kennedy permits himself to sneer at "some grand warfare of rival ideologies." Since he could not possibly mean that that global conflict has, somehow, bypassed our country, there is only one other thing that he could have meant: that, for us, the conflict is over and statism—a government-managed economy—has won.

"The differences today are mainly matters of degree," he stated. "And we cannot understand and attack our contemporary problems if we are bound by the traditional labels and worn-out slogans of an earlier era."

If we don't use any "labels"—which means: if we never identify the nature of different political systems we will not discover that we are accepting statism, or notice how that switch is pulled on us.

"The solid ground of mutual confidence," said Mr. Kennedy, "is the necessary partnership of government with all the sectors of our society in the steady quest for economic progress."

"Partnership" is an indecent euphemism for "government control."

There can be no partnership between armed bureaucrats and defenseless private citizens who have no choice but to obey.

Government control over "all sectors of a society" is the essence of statism in any of its forms: Fascism, Communism, Nazism, Socialism, and any "mixed" economy on its sliding way to one of those major four. "The differences are mainly matters of degree."

No, Mr. Kennedy does not believe that the ideological switch has already been accomplished. That is what his speech was striving to accomplish. It is on the last, transitional lap of that fatal slide that it becomes important to silence ideological discussions.

Mr. Kennedy's speech was part of an increasingly apparent attempt to pull an intellectual coup d'état.

Mr. Kennedy and his advisers seem determined to cash in on our philosophical and cultural bankruptcy, on the cowardice of their opponents, on the default of the so-called "conservatives" who evade basic issues and haggle only over trivial details. An intellectual coup d'état would consist of taking over a vacuum, in the following manner: keep switching the meaning of political concepts until they dissolve in an unintelligible fog—get people conditioned subliminally to accept the implications of the doctrines you would not dare proclaim explicitly—then let them wake up some morning to a fait accompli, to the astonished realization: "Why, everybody knows that freedom is slavery and that Americanism is statism."

Such, apparently, is the planned attempt. Those who fall for it, deserve it. Those who do not, should make their protest heard.

The Cold Civil War

JULY 22,1962—A "mixed economy" is a society in the process of committing suicide.

If a nation cannot survive half-slave, half-free, consider the condition of a nation in which every social group becomes both the slave and the enslaver of every other group. Ask yourself how long such a condition can last and what is its inevitable outcome.

When government controls are introduced into a free economy, they create economic dislocations, hardships and problems, which—if the controls are not repealed—necessitate further controls, which necessitate still further controls, etc. Thus a chain reaction is set up: the victimized groups seek redress by imposing controls on the profiteering groups, who retaliate in the same manner, on an ever-widening scale.

A man who is tied cannot run a race against men who are free: he must either demand that his bonds be removed or that all the other contestants be tied as well. If men choose the second, the economic race slows down to a walk, then to a stagger, then to a crawl—and then they all collapse at the goal posts of a Very Old Frontier: the totalitarian state. No one is the winner but the government.

This process is known as "a declining rate of economic growth."

We are nearing the climax of this process and can watch it in the daily headlines. Every group in turn is beginning to show signs of panic, sensing its peril. But what policy do they all follow?

When Secretary Goldberg announced, during the steel industry's contract negotiations, that the government had arrogated to itself the exclusive right to "define and assert the national interest" in issues of collective bargaining—labor leaders protested swiftly and properly. George Meany [president of the A.F.L.-C.I.O.] declared: "When he says the role of the government is to assert the national interest, he is infringing on the rights of free people and free society. . . ."

What was industry's answer? The N.A.M. [National Association of Manufacturers] issued a cautious protest, with the following advice: "The real remedy is to subject labor organizations to legal restrictions on the attainment and use of monopoly power."

Instead of seeking an alliance against their common enemy, and attempting to break the chains of the antitrust laws, which are choking it, industry was demanding that these laws be extended to chain the only powerful contestant who is still semi-free.

When the doctors began their desperate fight against socialized medicine, George Meany was among those present at Mr. Kennedy's circus in Madison Square Garden, inaugurating the propaganda drive for the enslavement of the medical profession.

Organized labor supports "Medicare," giving, apparently, no thought to the fact that once the professions are enslaved, there will be no conceivable way for labor to retain any freedom.

While the doctors are putting up a heroic and, so far, successful fight—proving that it can be done—the root of future defeats is in their own camp. The voices of most of their official spokesmen, such as the A.M.A. [American Medical Association], are almost as cautiously middle-roadish as the voice of the N.A.M. They seem to treat the issue exclusively as a narrow problem of their own profession, carefully avoiding any reference to wider political principles or issues.

The significant exception to that policy is the attitude of the doctors in New Jersey who acted like men and declared that they would not cooperate with their own enslavement.

If any representatives of industry raised their voices in support of the medical profession, I have not heard them. As to the voices of the press, they were predominantly on the side of the government.

Some time ago, when Mr. Kennedy suggested, vaguely and tentatively, that newspapers ought to withhold such news as might be contrary to the "public interest," the newspapers were properly alarmed and expressed opposition to that hint. But when [F.C.C. chairman] Mr. Minow proposed to censor TV and radio by means of license-revoking, most of the press hailed him as a courageous crusader for culture and art.

When Mr. Kennedy forced the steel industry to obey his wishes without any legal authority to do so, by threatening to use the enormous, destructive, undefined and undefinable powers of the antitrust laws many people, including some of the better liberals, grasped the authoritarian nature of that performance. A great shudder of apprehension ran through the country, culminating in the stock market crash.

But has anyone proposed the revision, clarification or repeal of the antitrust laws to eliminate their grant of arbitrary powers to the government? No. Several bills are coming up, proposing to enlarge those powers.

Such is the nature of that "cold civil war" which is known as a "mixed economy." While every social group is destroying every other, the government waits on the sidelines, merely playing favorites and growing. No matter who loses any particular battle, only totalitarian statism can win that war.

What is needed now is the emergence of men, within all social groups, who would rise above the worm's eye view of their immediate problems to a bird's eye view of the total situation. Such men would be statesmen, rather than politicians (the difference consists of the ability to grasp political principles). They would compute the terrible price of seeking governmental favors, they would see their common danger—and, perhaps, would initiate a process, not of chaining one another, but of trading de-control for de-control. No statist bureaucrats could withstand a united front of that kind.

Government by Intimidation

JULY 29,1962 —"In the F.C.C. and in the Antitrust Division the government possesses the legal weapons it needs to transform this country into a totalitarian state—and if the 'conservatives' do not know it, the present Administration seems to know it."

When I wrote this, in the first number of *The Objectivist Newsletter*, in January, 1962, I pointed out that these were the two crucially dangerous issues, which advocates of freedom had to fight. I could not foresee how swiftly the Administration would proceed on that course.

On July 15, *The New York Times* carried a story announcing: "An antitrust panel of the House Judiciary Committee is preparing a broad inquiry on the press and other news media."

To understand what this means, one must bear in mind that the antitrust laws are not laws in any normal, civilized sense of the word. They are an accumulation of non-objective, undefinable, unjudicable statutes, so contradictory and inconsistent that no two jurists can agree on their meaning, and any business practice can be construed as illegal. Thus the government has the power to prosecute and to convict any business concern it chooses.

Consider what will happen to the freedom of the press when that sort of noose tightens about its necks and its typewriters.

Representative Emanuel Celler is in charge of the coming inquiry. *The New York Times* quotes him as declaring: "We are very much aware of the First Amendment. We are also aware that the courts have said you can distinguish between the business practices and the editorial operations of newspapers."

Apparently, Mr. Celler regarded a declaration of his "awareness" as sufficient compliance with the Constitution—because he then proceeded to announce that the inquiry will deal with such (non-editorial?) issues as the "handling of news and the impact of syndicated columns on the gathering and presentation of local news."

Mr. Celler will also investigate the fact that in some cities one man or company owns both the morning and evening newspapers.

"We shall endeavor to find out," he stated, "whether, in those cities, the news is slanted according to the prejudice or idiosyncrasies of those common owners; whether the editorial policy is consistently

21

politically slanted." (A non-editorial issue?)

Does this mean that the owner of a newspaper has no right to hold "consistent" political convictions and that a newspaper is not entitled to a "consistent" editorial policy? If the owner of one newspaper possesses the right of free speech, does he lose it if he acquires two newspapers? Who determines what is "slanted" and which political views are "prejudice or idiosyncrasies"? The government?

The only mergers Mr. Celler cited as under investigation are recent purchases of newspapers by S. I. Newhouse and by the Hearst Publishing Company. Both these newspaper chains are not exactly "liberal" in their political views nor overly friendly to the Administration.

"Also," declared Mr. Celler, "we are interested in seeing whether or to what extent the columnists might be drying up local talent in assaying the news of the day."

Well, it is incontestably certain that the talents of the local "High School Bugle" could not possibly compete with nationally syndicated columnists.

Here we see the essence of the antitrust doctrines—in so grotesque a form that no satirist would venture to offer it as a caricature. Yet it is not a caricature, it is the naked, brutal truth.

If it is right to sacrifice ability to incompetence, or success to failure, or achievement to envy—if it is right to break up giant industrial concerns because smaller companies cannot compete with them—then it is right to silence every man who has acquired a national audience and clear the field for those whose audience will never grow beyond the corner drugstore.

If it is right to deprive the small towns of the wider choice and lower prices offered by the big chain stores, and force them to support the "little corner grocer"—then it is right to deprive them of any intellectual contact with the nation, of any famous voices, of any TV network programs, and confine them by law to the news of local Rummage Sales and Ice Cream Socials, to the "assaying" of such news by cracker-barrel pundits, and to the poetry recitals of the League of Mrs. Worthington's Daughters.

Freedom of speech? "Why, we don't deprive any man of his freedom of speech," the trustbusters would chorus, "provided he is not heard beyond the boundaries of his township or of his city block."

No, the government would not establish any censorship; it would not need to. The threat of antitrust prosecutions will be sufficient. We have seen what it did to the steel industry. Rule by hidden, unprovable intimidation relies on the victims' "voluntary" self-enslavement. The result is worse than a censored press; it is a servile press.

Consider the significance of a curious contradiction. On the one hand, the government hails the launching of Telstar as a means of uniting the whole world in a single network of global communication. On the other hand, the government proposes to disintegrate national communications into local atoms, forbidding any private individual to acquire the means of addressing the nation, and forbidding the separate atoms to know what the rest of the nation is thinking.

Do you grasp the possibilities?

President Kennedy is to broadcast his news conferences via Telstar. Which one of us will obtain equal time on that global medium? And if we do not, how will we make ourselves heard? It is not by means of the "High School Bugle" that one can protect one's rights or compete with a monopoly of that kind.

Gentlemen of the press, if any, now is the time to speak up.

Let Us Alone!

AUGUST 5,1962—Since "economic growth" is today's great problem, and government economists seem baffled by our declining rate of growth, I wonder how many people know the origin of the term "laissez-faire"?

France, in the 17th century, was an absolute monarchy. Her system has been described as "absolutism limited by chaos." The King held total power over everyone's life, work and property—and only the corruption of government officials gave people an unofficial margin of freedom.

Louis XIV was an archetypical despot: a pretentious mediocrity with grandiose ambitions. His reign is considered one of the brilliant periods of French history: he provided the country with a "national goal," in the form of long and successful wars; he established France as the leading power and the cultural center of Europe. But "national goals" cost money. The fiscal policies of his government led to a chronic state of crisis, solved by the immemorial expedient of draining the country through ever-increasing taxation.

Colbert, chief adviser of Louis XIV, was one of the early modern statists. Believing that government regulations can create national prosperity and that higher tax revenues can be obtained only from the country's "economic growth," he devoted himself to seeking "a general increase in wealth by the encouragement of industry." His method consisted of establishing countless government controls and minute regulations that choked business activity; the result was dismal failure.

Colbert was not an enemy of business; no more than is President Kennedy. Colbert was eager to help fatten the sacrificial victims—and on one historical occasion, he asked a group of manufacturers what he could do for industry. A manufacturer named Legendre answered: "Laissez-nous faire!" "Let us alone!"

Apparently, the French businessmen of the 17th century had more courage than their American counterparts of the 20th, and a better understanding of economics. They knew that government "help" to business is just as disastrous as government persecution, and that the only way a government can be of service to national prosperity is by keeping its hands off.

To say that that which was true in the 17th century cannot possibly be true today, because we travel in jet planes while they traveled in horse carts—is like saying that modern men do not need food, as men did in the past, because they are wearing trenchcoats and slacks, instead of powdered wigs and hoop skirts. It is that sort of concrete-bound superficiality—or inability to distinguish the essential from the non-essential—that blinds people to the fact that the economic crisis of our day is the oldest and stalest one in history.

Consider the essentials. If government controls could achieve nothing but paralysis, starvation and collapse in a pre-industrial age, what happens when one imposes controls on a highly industrialized economy? Which is easier for bureaucrats to regulate: the operation of hand looms and hand forges—or the operation of an electronics industry, with the incalculable number of men of creative intelligence required to build and to maintain it?

Regardless of the purpose for which one intends to use it, wealth must first be produced. As far as economics is concerned, there is no difference between the motives of Colbert and of President Kennedy. Both wanted to achieve national prosperity. Whether the wealth extorted by taxation is drained for the unearned benefit of Louis XIV or for the unearned benefit of the "underprivileged" makes no difference to the economic productivity of a nation. Whether one is chained for a "noble" purpose or an ignoble one, for the benefit of the rich or the poor, for the sake of somebody's "greed" or somebody's "need"—when one is chained, one cannot produce.

There is no difference in the ultimate fate of all chained economies, regardless of any alleged justifications for the chains.

The creation of "consumer demand"? It would be interesting to compute how many housewives with relief checks would equal the "consumer demands" provided by Madame de Maintenon and her numerous colleagues.

A "fair" distribution of wealth? The privileged favorites of Louis XIV did not enjoy so unfair an advantage over other people as do our "aristocrats of pull," the actual and potential variants of Billie Sol Estes.

The requirements of the "national interest"? If there is such a thing as a "national interest" achieved by sacrificing the interests of individual citizens, then Louis XIV acquitted himself superlatively. The greater part of his extravagance was not "selfish": he did build France up into a major international power—and wrecked her economy.

The furtherance of our "cultural" or "spiritual" progress? It is doubtful that a government-subsidized W.P.A. theater project will ever produce an array of genius comparable to that supported by the court of Louis XIV in his role of "patron of the arts" (Corneille, Racine, Molière, etc.).

The fact is that motives do not alter facts. The paramount requirement of a nation's productivity and prosperity is freedom; men cannot—and, morally, will not—produce under compulsion and controls.

There is nothing mysterious about the present crisis of our economy. Like Colbert, President Kennedy is appealing to various economic groups, seeking advice on what he can do for them. And if he does not wish to go down in history with a record similar to Colbert's, he would do well to heed the voice of a modern Legendre, if such exists, who could give him the same immortal advice in a single word: "De-control!"

Just Suppose

AUGUST 12,1962—Wouldn't it be wonderful if we had an opposition party that really wanted to win this fall's elections? To hope that the Republican Party might want to would require, perhaps, that one stretch one's imagination a bit too far. So let us just call it Party X—and let us suppose what such a party would do.

Party X would oppose statism and would advocate free enterprise. But it would know that one cannot win anybody's support by repeating that slogan until it turns into a stale, hypocritical platitude—while simultaneously accepting and endorsing every step in the growth of government controls.

Party X would know that opposition does not consist of declaring to the voters: "The Administration plans to tighten the leash around your throats until you choke—but we're lovers of freedom and we're opposed to it, so we'll tighten it only a couple of inches."

Party X would not act as Exhibit A for its enemies, when they charge that it is passive, stagnant, "me-tooing" and has no solutions for the country's problems. It would offer the voters concrete solutions and specific proposals, based on the principles of free enterprise. The opportunities to do so are countless, and Party X would not miss them.

For instance:

President Kennedy has announced that he will use the defeat of "Medicare" as an issue in the coming campaign. He declared that it was "a most serious defeat for every American family," not merely for the aged, but for "all those Americans who have parents, who are liable to be ill, and who have children to educate at the same time, mothers and fathers in their thirties and forties."

Party X would not miss a challenge of that kind. It would demand to know why these families—who carry a heavy share of the welfare state's burden—are not allowed a tax exemption on the money they spend for their children's education. And Party X would offer this proposal to the voters: a tax exemption for the educational expenses of all citizens.

Party X would declare that if any political leader's motive were concern for the rights and problems of individual citizens—rather than

27

a desire to use their plight as a pretext for expanding the government's power—the outrageous tax situation of today would not be permitted to exist.

On the one hand, education is acclaimed as the country's vital need and the government proposes to spend millions of tax dollars under the so-called "Aid to Education" program. On the other hand, the great majority of hard-working families, from whom those taxes are squeezed, cannot afford to give their children a college education, or can do so only at the price of real hardships—yet they are not allowed to deduct educational costs from the taxable income of their meager budgets.

On the one hand, the government professes concern over the young people who drop out of school because they cannot afford to continue their education. On the other hand, the young people who struggle to work their way through school are forced to pay taxes on the desper-ately insufficient earnings which they spend to equip themselves by their own effort for a productive career.

On the one hand, the government has just passed a bill to spend millions of tax dollars to retrain workers for new jobs. On the other hand, look at the night schools where adults of all ages are striving to study, after a full workday, willing to spend eight years on a four-year college course—and you will have to feel that the taxes they pay are indeed blood money.

Party X would have the courage to defend those defenseless victims: the self-supporting.

It would propose: (a) that all educational expenses of all citizens be made tax exempt, and (b) that private citizens be allowed tax exemptions on the money they may spend to help the education of an individual of their own choice.

Knowing that a cut in taxes should be accompanied by a corresponding cut in government spending, Party X would compute the costs and choose the specific government projects it would promise to abolish. If the country heard some concrete details of what those taxes are spent on—such as the story of a few foreign lobbies—anyone but a confirmed totalitarian would scream in protest.

Party X would set the pattern for the gradual lifting of the tax burden—at a time when both business and labor are beginning to realize that the best way to save a collapsing economy is to leave more of their own money to the citizens who earned it.

Such would be Party X's answer to some current problems: it would aid education, send the "drop-outs" back to school, and diminish unemployment through the jobs thus vacated.

This is just one example, one of the countless possibilities open to a party that would detect the groping new trend to freedom and become its pacemaker.

Party X would realize that such a program would marshal the support of the greatest "pressure group" in the world: the middle class— the productive, self-supporting men who have never been organized into a pressure group, because it is they who pay the costs of all the statist schemes, and their interests could be defended only by a true free-enterprise party, if such existed.

There is no Party X. But there are, perhaps, some practical politicians among the Republicans, who might realize that a stand of this kind would win. And, perhaps, there are even a few idealists who might care that it would also save the country.

Through Your Most Grievous Fault

AUGUST 19,1962—The death of Marilyn Monroe shocked people, with an impact different from their reaction to the death of any other movie star or public figure. All over the world people felt a peculiar sense of personal involvement and of protest, like a universal cry of "Oh, no!"

They felt that her death had some special significance, almost like a warning which they could not decipher—and they felt a nameless apprehension, the sense that something terribly wrong was involved.

They were right to feel it.

Marilyn Monroe, on the screen, was an image of pure, innocent, childlike joy in living. She projected the sense of a person born and reared in some radiant Utopia, untouched by suffering, unable to conceive of ugliness or evil, facing life with the confidence, the benevolence and the joyous self-flaunting of a child or a kitten who is happy to display its own attractiveness as the best gift it can offer the world, and who expects to be admired for it, not hurt.

In real life, Marilyn Monroe's suicide—or worse: a suicide that might have been an accident, suggesting that, to her, the difference did not matter—was a declaration that we live in a world which made it impossible for her kind of spirit, and for the things she represented, to survive.

If there ever was a victim of society, Marilyn Monroe was that victim—of a society that professes dedication to the relief of the suffering, but kills the joyous.

None of the objects of the humanitarians' tender solicitude, the juvenile delinquents, could have had so sordid and horrifying a childhood as did Marilyn Monroe.

To survive it and to preserve the kind of spirit she projected on the screen—the radiantly benevolent sense of life, which cannot be faked—was an almost inconceivable psychological achievement that required a heroism of the highest order. Whatever scars her past had left were insignificant by comparison.

She preserved her vision of life through a nightmare struggle, fighting her way to the top. What broke her was the discovery, at the top, of as sordid an evil as the one she had left behind—worse, perhaps, because incomprehensible. She had expected to reach the sunlight; she found, instead, a limitless swamp of malice.

It was a malice of a very special kind. If you want to see her groping struggle to understand it, read the magnificent article in a recent issue of *Life* magazine. It is not actually an article, it is a verbatim transcript of her own words—and the most tragically revealing document published in many years. It is a cry for help, which came too late to be answered.

"When you're famous, you kind of run into human nature in a raw kind of way," she said. "It stirs up envy, fame does. People you run into feel that, well, who is she—who does she think she is, Marilyn Monroe? They feel fame gives them some kind of privilege to walk up to you and say anything to you, you know, of any kind of nature—and it won't hurt your feelings—like it's happening to your clothing. . . . I don't understand why people aren't a little more generous with each other. I don't like to say this, but I'm afraid there is a lot of envy in this business."

"Envy" is the only name she could find for the monstrous thing she faced, but it was much worse than envy: it was the profound hatred of life, of success and of all human values, felt by a certain kind of mediocrity—the kind who feels pleasure on hearing about a stranger's misfortune. It was hatred of the good for being the good—hatred of ability, of beauty, of honesty, of earnestness, of achievement and, above all, of human joy.

Read the *Life* article to see how it worked and what it did to her:

An eager child, who was rebuked for her eagerness—"Sometimes the [foster] families used to worry because I used to laugh so loud and so gay; I guess they felt it was hysterical."

A spectacularly successful star, whose employers kept repeating: "Remember you're not a star," in a determined effort, apparently, not to let her discover her own importance.

A brilliantly talented actress, who was told by the alleged authorities, by Hollywood, by the press, that she could not act.

An actress, dedicated to her art with passionate earnestness—"When I was 5—I think that's when I started wanting to be an actress—I loved to play. I didn't like the world around me because it was kind of grim—

but I loved to play house and it was like you could make your own boundaries"—who went through hell to make her own boundaries, to offer people the sunlit universe of her own vision—"It's almost having certain kinds of secrets for yourself that you'll let the whole world in on only for a moment, when you're acting"—but who was ridiculed for her desire to play serious parts.

A woman, the only one, who was able to project the glowingly innocent sexuality of a being from some planet uncorrupted by guilt— who found herself regarded and ballyhooed as a vulgar symbol of obscenity—and who still had the courage to declare: "We are all born sexual creatures, thank God, but it's a pity so many people despise and crush this natural gift."

A happy child who was offering her achievement to the world, with the pride of an authentic greatness and of a kitten depositing a hunting trophy at your feet—who found herself answered by concerted efforts to negate, to degrade, to ridicule, to insult, to destroy her achievement—who was unable to conceive that it was her best she was punished for, not her worst—who could only sense, in helpless terror, that she was facing some unspeakable kind of evil.

How long do you think a human being could stand it?

That hatred of values has always existed in some people, in any age or culture. But a hundred years ago, they would have been expected to hide it. Today, it is all around us; it is the style and fashion of our century.

Where would a sinking spirit find relief from it?

The evil of a cultural atmosphere is made by all those who share it. Anyone who has ever felt resentment against the good for being the good and has given voice to it, is the murderer of Marilyn Monroe.

An Open Letter To My Readers

AUGUST 26, 1962—In his column of July 29, Mr. Nick B. Williams, editor of the *Los Angeles Times*, mentioned that he was swamped with letters about my column and that "the count has been running solidly for Miss Rand."

I want to say "thank you" to all those readers who wrote expressing support of my stand. Although my acknowledgment has to be in a "collective" form, I am addressing it individually to each one of you.

You have helped me to prove once more a conviction of mine which is shared by few of today's "intellectuals," namely: that the public does think.

From the start of my career, the issue I found hardest to fight—harder than the opposition of sundry leftists—was the blind, malevolent stubbornness of men who kept telling me that my work was too intellectual and that "the public doesn't think." I have heard it from men in every medium of communication: from book publishers, from stage, screen, TV and radio producers, from newspapermen, from professors, from politicians.

There are many different reasons for their attitude, some innocent, some not. The innocent error comes from the bitterness of men who have seen too many instances of human irrationality. The guilty attitude is that of men who blame "the public" as an excuse for their own bad taste and bad judgment.

No, the public is not always right. "The public" is only a number of individuals, and every individual may be right or wrong. But nothing is more contemptible than the willingness to pander to human stupidity and ignore human intelligence, regardless of the numerical preponderance of either at any given time.

For years, I have been arguing that the general public is much more intelligent than its alleged leaders give it credit for; that people do care for ideas and are searching desperately for the spokesmen of reason; that only reason can work, though not always immediately; and that the evidence of it, on a historical scale, is the fact that no dictatorship can last without the help of censorship—because, in a free marketplace of ideas, truth and reason will always win.

Thank you for one more demonstration of it.

33

I have been receiving an increasing number of letters, asking many questions about Objectivism—more questions than I can answer by mail. So I shall indicate where the answers may be obtained. I am addressing myself to those who are genuinely interested in ideas and who, therefore, have an authentic desire to understand Objectivism. "Those who're making an effort to fail to understand me, are not a concern of mine."

[Miss Rand then indicates courses and other materials on her philosophy available at the time. She concludes with the following note about those who misrepresent her ideas.]

Some of the misrepresentations may be unintentional, since some people find it difficult to grasp new ideas, let alone to summarize them correctly. But most of the misrepresentations are deliberate, since an attempt to ascribe to a writer the exact opposite of her ideas can hardly be attributed to an innocent error. There are many such attempts, some of them recent and close at hand. Those who credit them, deserve them.

On a television interview, Mike Wallace once asked me what I thought of such tactics. I answered that I agree with a line of advice from Kipling's poem "If": "if you can bear to hear the truth you've spoken twisted by knaves to make a trap for fools. . . ." I can bear it. It is not fools that I seek to address.

Mickey Spillane

SEPTEMBER 2,1962—Mickey Spillane is one of the best writers of our time. He has won an enormous popular following—but no acknowledgment. He stands as a measure of the gulf between the public and its alleged intellectual leaders.

Being the most popular, he has suffered the most vicious injustice on the part of the "intellectuals"—which is a clue to their psychology and to the state of our culture. Like "The Untouchables," like any outstanding exponent of the Romantic school of art, he has been subjected to a sustained campaign of smears, attacks and denunciations—not for errors, but for achievements, not for flaws, but for his artistic virtues.

Most of today's "intellectuals"—the statist collectivists, the worshippers of "the masses," the servants of "the people"—are savagely antagonistic to the people's standards and to every authentic, popular value in art.

They feel hatred for any projection of man as a clean, self-confident, efficacious being. They extol depravity; they relish the sight of man spitting in his own face. The object of their deepest hatred (and fear) is moral values. Their view of life is best symbolized by a middle-aged professor who seduces a twelve-year old girl—and whose story is treated humorously.

It is absurd that the same aesthetes, who acclaim the above obscenity as "adult" and "artistic," should voice concern over the "immoral" influence of Mickey Spillane.

They allege that "sex and violence" are the cause of his popular appeal. What they hate him for is the fact that Mickey Spillane is an intransigent moral crusader.

Detective fiction presents, in simple, primitive essentials, the conflict of good and evil; that is the root of its appeal. Mickey Spillane is a moral absolutist. His characterizations are excellent and drawn in black-and-whites; there are no slippery half-tones, no cowardly evasions, no cynicism—and no forgiveness; there are no doubts about the evil of evil.

Spillane's view of life has a strong element of tragic bitterness: he projects the belief that evil is powerful (a view with which I do not agree), but that man has the capacity to fight it and that no allowances, concessions or compromises are morally conceivable or possible (with which I do agree). His hero, Mike Hammer, is a moral avenger, passionately dedicated to justice, to the defense of the wronged and to the destruction of evil.

That bitter, but intensely moralistic view of life is the key to the secret of Mickey Spillane's unparalleled popularity throughout the world. He is the true voice of the people, in the twentieth century. Men everywhere feel trapped by the spread of an uncontested, incomprehensible evil. They have borne so much injustice, seen so many cynically indifferent faces and stored so much frustrated indignation, that the image of Mike Hammer becomes their embodied dream, like an answer to the cry for help they are too inarticulate to utter.

As a writer, Mickey Spillane has a brilliant literary talent. Few modern writers can approach his originality, his imagination, his sense of drama, the ingenuity of his plot-structures. His style is uneven, not yet fully disciplined; but his best passages are literarily superior to the work of most of today's so-called "serious" writers.

All these values can be enjoyed again in *The Girl Hunters*—a new novel by Mickey Spillane, which brings Mike Hammer back after an absence of ten years. It will be published on September 27.

One expects the unexpected from Mickey Spillane—and one gets it. The story opens with Mike Hammer as a drunken bum who has gone to pieces under the pressure of self-reproach for a tragic disaster. What caused it and what brings him back, you will have to find out for yourself.

Though beautifully written and extremely dramatic, Mike Hammer as a bum is somewhat out of character (and here is one admirer of Mike's who objects to it)—but, fortunately, his recovery is fairly speedy. It is also somewhat out of character for Mickey Spillane to keep reminding Mike that he's not what he used to be—because he is. Both of them are. The old vitality, the energy, the pace, the excitement come breaking through, almost in spite of the author's intention. I almost wish Mike would tell Mickey that it would take a much worse man than he, Mickey, is, to keep Mike Hammer down.

The Girl Hunters is not fully up to the standard of Spillane's best novels, *The Long Wait* and *One Lonely Night*. It is marred by an oddly inconclusive ending, after a brilliantly sustained suspense. The mystery is solved, but the story is not fully consummated dramatically; it seems to demand a sequel—and if this was the author's intention, then he fully succeeded in arousing the readers' interest.

There is a certain air of maturity about this novel, which is both a virtue and a flaw. It is a virtue in respect to Spillane's style, which has become more polished and more controlled. It is a flaw in respect to a certain stress of bitterness: a faint over-concern with the psychology of hatred, a faint dimming of adventurous enjoyment.

"Maturity" is a slightly disturbing concept when applied to Spillane. Maturity of technique is always a value. But maturity of spirit can have many meanings, some of them undesirable. And in spirit—in the sense of life they have created, in their exuberant energy, in the spontaneous enthusiasm they project and evoke—both Mike Hammer and Mickey Spillane should remain timelessly young.

The Dying Victim of Berlin

SEPTEMBER 9, 1962—Those who do not understand the process by which the morality of altruism is destroying the world, may observe it in the disgraceful nightmare of America's foreign policy.

We are draining our life-blood—our economic power—on the sacrificial altar of global needs, asking nothing in return. Allegedly, what we expect to gain is the friendship of other nations. But we are betraying the friendly nations that trust us—we are destroying the recipients of our help—and we are delivering the world into the power of the very evil we are calling men to fight.

We are proclaiming that it is our duty to lead a world crusade against communism—and we are destroying its only opposite, the only system that can fight it: our own.

This is the essence of altruism: the first sacrifice it demands—of a man or of a nation—is the abandonment of self-esteem.

In a recent interview with a group of Brazilian university students, President Kennedy made it clear that we have no direction to offer the world, no political principles, no ideals, no goals. He declared that socialism was as acceptable to us as any other system. "If by socialization you mean ownership of the means of production or of the basic industries," he said, "that is a judgment which you must make. . . . We prefer the competitive market economy here. . . . You may decide that or you may decide on another course of action. We would accept that as long as it represented a free choice."

I quote two definitions from *The American College Dictionary.*

"Communism: a theory or system of social organization based on the holding of all property in common, actual ownership being ascribed to the community as a whole or to the state."

"Socialism: a theory or system of social organization which advocates the vesting of ownership and control of the means of production, capital, land, etc. in the community as a whole."

Is this what we are asked to crusade, sacrifice, fight and die for?

There is no difference between communism and socialism, except in the means of achieving the same ultimate end: communism proposes to enslave men by force, socialism—by vote. It is merely the difference between murder and suicide.

The uniquely, specifically American political principle was the Rights of Man—not the Rights of Mob.

The American system, based on the rights of the individual, was capitalism. Freedom, progress, prosperity and all the other values of a civilized society were the product of capitalism and have never existed (nor can ever be maintained) under any other system.

But it is capitalism that our statist-collectivist intellectuals reject—and our foreign policy is the monument to the bankruptcy of their leadership.

People the world over understand the nature of the global conflict, even though their leaders do not have the courage to name it: individual rights versus brute force—freedom versus slavery—capitalism versus socialism.

By condemning, denouncing and apologizing for her own system, America is disarming them intellectually and killing their only hope.

Soviet Russia does not need to do much propaganda about altruism or about the "right" of the "underprivileged" to everybody else's property—we are doing it for her. She is cashing in on our ideological suicide, secure in the knowledge that communism is the most consistent political embodiment of altruism—of general self-sacrifice—and that the crude brutality of her conquests will encounter no resistance.

Which side will the people of the world choose in such circumstances—particularly those new nations, emerging from savagery, who understand nothing but the power of brute force?

The gullible, sentimental collectivists of the West are puzzled by Russia's current atrocities. They are wondering why Russia does not seem to care about the public opinion of the world, why she is dropping her humanitarian "image" and showing her naked soul in such acts as the detonation of the biggest nuclear bomb, the erection of the concentration-camp wall in Berlin, the sadistic horror of shooting fleeing children. Those Western parlor-pinks miss the nature of the message that Russia is conveying to the world.

The message is the boast of a brute, deliberately defying every value of civilization, every vestige of respect for human life and rights, proving that their champions are impotent to defend them—and thus declaring to the uncivilized hordes of the globe that the world is theirs to take over.

This is the purpose of shooting an eighteen-year old boy who tried to escape from East Berlin, and letting him bleed to death at the foot of the wall, in the sight and hearing of the Western people.

West Germany is the freest, the most nearly capitalist economy in Europe. The contrast between West and East Berlin is the most eloquent modern evidence of the superiority of capitalism over communism. The evidence is irrefutable. Russia does not intend to refute it. She is staging an ideological showdown: she is spitting in our face and declaring that might is right, that brutality is more powerful than all our principles, our promises, our ideals, our wealth and our incomparable material superiority.

Such is the silent symbol now confronting the world: the steel skyscrapers, the glowing shop windows, the glittering cars, the lights of West Berlin—the achievement of capitalism and of capitalism's essence: of free, individual men—and, lying on its doorstep, in the outer darkness, the bleeding body of a single, individual man who had wanted to be free.

Soviet Russia understands the heart of the issue.

When are we going to begin to understand it?

Ninety-Three

SEPTEMBER 16,1962 —"Then, without haste, slowly, proudly, he stepped over the window sill, and, not turning, standing straight, his back against the rungs of the ladder, with the flames behind him and the abyss ahead, he began to descend the ladder in silence with the majesty of a phantom. . . .With each step he made toward the men whose eyes, aghast, stared at him through the darkness, he seemed to grow taller. . . .

"When he came down, when he had reached the last rung of the ladder and placed his foot on the ground, a hand fell on his shoulder. He turned.

" 'I arrest you,' said—

" 'You are right.' . . ."

I heard this scene when I was seven years old, lying awake in the darkness, listening intently to a voice reading aloud behind the closed door of the nursery. It was my mother reading a French novel to my grandmother in the living room, and all I could hear was a few snatches. But they gave me the sense of some tremendous drama resolving events of unimaginable importance.

When people look back at their childhood or youth, their wistfulness comes from the memory, not of what their lives had been in those years, but of what life had then promised to be. The expectation of some undefinable splendor, of the unusual, the exciting, the great, is an attribute of youth—and the process of aging is the process of that expectation's gradual extinction.

One does not have to let it happen. But that fire dies for lack of fuel, under the gray weight of disappointments, when one discovers that the adults do not know what they are doing, nor care—that a person one respected is an abject coward—that a public figure one admired is a posturing mediocrity—that a literary classic one had looked forward to reading is a minute analysis of people one would not want to look at twice, like a study in depth of a mud puddle.

But there are exceptions.

I did not ask what book that scene came from, since I was not supposed to be listening. It remained in my mind as a brilliant flash; I did

41

not expect to find it again nor to learn the mystery of such questions as who was arrested and why.

I was thirteen when I found it, with a sudden shock of recognition, in the closing chapters of a magnificent novel. It was *Ninety-Three* by Victor Hugo.

That scene was not as good as I had thought—it was better. It was incomparably better than anything I could have imagined. It was the climax of so enormous a drama, the resolution of such profound moral conflicts, that it left one stunned by the experience of what great literature is really like; after which, one does not settle for any lesser values, neither in books nor in life.

Now, some forty years later, I was asked to write an introduction for a new translation of *Ninety-Three*. It has just been published, in paperback, by Bantam Books. I almost envy the readers who can discover Victor Hugo for the first time.

I quote from my introduction: "The distance between his world and ours is astonishingly short—he died in 1885—but the distance between his universe and ours has to be measured in esthetic light years. . . .He is as invisible to the neo-barbarians of our age as the art of Rome was to their spiritual ancestors, and for the same reasons. Yet Victor Hugo is the greatest novelist in world literature."

The background of *Ninety-Three* is the French Revolution. The title refers to 1793, the year of the terror. The theme is that which is most signally lacking in today's culture: man's loyalty to values.

Three figures dominate the violence of a ruthless civil war: an intransigent aristocrat, who leads a royalist rebellion against the revolution—his nephew and heir, a young revolutionary who commands the republican army sent to crush the rebellion—an ex-priest, now a dedicated leader of the revolution, who is sent to watch the political loyalty of the young commander, his former pupil, the only man he ever loved.

Their story is told, not by the sloppy stream of an unfocused consciousness, but by the purposeful drive of a focused mind, which means: by the mounting suspense of a brilliantly integrated plot-structure.

You may read any number of more "realistic" accounts of the French Revolution, but Hugo's is the one you will remember. He is not a reporter of the momentary, but an artist who projects the essential and fundamental. He is not a statistician of gutter trivia, but a Romanticist who presents life "as it might be and ought to be." He is the worshipper and the superlative portrayer of man's greatness.

If you are struggling to hold your vision of man above the gray ashes of our century, Hugo is the fuel you need.

One cannot preserve that vision or achieve it without some knowledge of what is greatness and some image to concretize it. Every morning, when you read today's headlines, you shrink a little in human stature and hope. Then, if you turn to modern literature for a nobler view of man, you are confronted by those cases of arrested development—the juvenile delinquents aged thirty to sixty—who still think that depravity is daring or shocking, and whose writing belongs, not on paper, but on fences.

If you feel, as I do, that there's nothing as boring as depravity, if you seek a glimpse of human grandeur—turn to a novel by Victor Hugo.

Blind Chaos

SEPTEMBER 23,1962—There is an important political lesson to be learned from the current events in Algeria.

President Kennedy, the product and spokesman of modern intellectual trends, has been waging an ideological war against ideology. He has been stating repeatedly that political philosophy is useless and that "sophistication" consists of acting on the expediency of the moment.

On July 31, he declared to a group of Brazilian students that there are no rules or principles governing "the means of providing progress" and that any political system is as good as any other, including socialism, as long as it represents "a free choice" of the people.

On August 31, just one month later, history—like a well-constructed play—gave him an eloquent answer. The people of Algiers marched through the streets of the city, in desperate protest against the new threat of civil war, shouting: "We want peace! We want a government!"

How are they to go about getting it?

Through the years of civil war, they had been united, not by any political philosophy, but only by a racial issue. They were fighting, not for any program, but only against French rule. When they won their independence, they fell apart—into rival tribes and armed "willayas" fighting one another.

The New York Times (September 2) described it as "a bitter scramble for power among the men who were expected to lead the country." But to lead it—where? In the absence of political principles, the issue of government is an issue of seizing power and ruling by brute force.

The people of Algeria and their various tribal chieftains, who represent the majority that fought the war against France, are being taken over by a well organized minority that did not appear on the scene until after the victory. That minority is led by Ben Bella and was armed by Soviet Russia.

A majority without an ideology is a helpless mob, to be taken over by anyone.

Now consider the meaning of Mr. Kennedy's advice to the Brazilians and to the world. It was not the political philosophy of the United States that he was enunciating, but the principle of unlimited majority

44

rule—the doctrine that the majority may choose anything it wishes, that anything done by the majority is right and practical, because its will is omnipotent.

This means that the majority may vote away the rights of a minority—and dispose of an individual's life, liberty and property, until such time, if ever, as he is able to gather his own majority gang. This, somehow, will guarantee political freedom.

But wishing won't make it so—neither for an individual nor for a nation. Political freedom requires much more than the people's wish. It requires an enormously complex knowledge of political theory and of how to implement it in practice.

It took centuries of intellectual, philosophical development to achieve political freedom. It was a long struggle, stretching from Aristotle to John Locke to the Founding Fathers. The system they established was not based on unlimited majority rule, but on its opposite: on individual rights, which were not to be alienated by majority vote or minority plotting. The individual was not left at the mercy of his neighbors or his leaders: the Constitutional system of checks and balances was scientifically devised to protect him from both.

This was the great American achievement—and if concern for the actual welfare of other nations were our present leaders' motive, this is what we should have been teaching the world.

Instead, we are deluding the ignorant and the semi-savage by telling them that no political knowledge is necessary—that our system is only a matter of subjective preference—that any prehistorical form of tribal tyranny, gang rule and slaughter will do just as well, with our sanction and support.

It is thus that we encourage the spectacle of Algerian workers marching through the streets and shouting the demand: "Work, not blood!"— without knowing what great knowledge and virtue are required to achieve it.

In the same way, in 1917, the Russian peasants were demanding: "Land and Freedom!" But Lenin and Stalin is what they got.

In 1933, the Germans were demanding: "Room to live!" But what they got was Hitler.

In 1793, the French were shouting: "Liberty, Equality, Fraternity!" What they got was Napoleon.

In 1776, the Americans were proclaiming "The Rights of Man"—and, led by political philosophers, they achieved it.

No revolution, no matter how justified, and no movement, no matter how popular, has ever succeeded without a political philosophy to guide it, to set its direction and goal.

The United States—history's magnificent example of a country created by political theorists—has abandoned its own philosophy and is falling apart. As a nation, we are splintering into warring tribes which—only by the fading momentum of a civilized tradition—are "economic pressure groups," at present. As opposition to our growing statism, we have nothing but the futile "willayas" of the so-called "conservatives," who are fighting, not for any political principles, but only against the "liberals."

Embittered by Algeria's collapse into chaos, one of her leaders remarked: "We used to laugh at the Congolese; now it goes for us."

And it goes for us, as well.

The Man-Haters

SEPTEMBER 30,1962—Few errors are as naive and suicidal as the attempts of the "conservatives" to justify capitalism on altruist-collectivist grounds.

Many people believe that altruism means kindness, benevolence or respect for the rights of others. But it means the exact opposite: it teaches self-sacrifice, as well as the sacrifice of others, to any unspecified "public need"; it regards man as a sacrificial animal.

Believing that collectivists are motivated by an authentic concern for the welfare of mankind, capitalism's alleged defenders assure its enemies that capitalism is the practical road to the socialists' goal, the best means to the same end, the best "servant" of public needs.

Then they wonder why they fail—and why the bloody muck of socialization keeps oozing forward over the face of the globe.

They fail, because no one's welfare can be achieved by anyone's sacrifice—and because man's welfare is not the socialists' goal. It is not for its alleged flaws that the altruist-collectivists hate capitalism, but for its virtues.

If you doubt it, consider a few examples.

Many collectivist historians criticize the Constitution of the United States on the ground that its authors were rich landowners who, allegedly, were motivated, not by any political ideals, but only by their own selfish economic interests.

This, of course, is not true. But it is true that capitalism does not require the sacrifice of anyone's interests. And what is significant here is the nature of the morality behind the collectivists' argument.

Prior to the American Revolution, through centuries of feudalism and monarchy, the interests of the rich lay in the expropriation, enslavement and misery of the rest of the people. A society, therefore, where the interests of the rich require general freedom, unrestricted productiveness and the protection of individual rights, should have been hailed as an ideal system by anyone whose goal is man's well-being.

But that is not the collectivists' goal.

A similar criticism is voiced by collectivist ideologists about the American Civil War. The North, they claim disparagingly, was motivated, not by self-sacrificial concern for the plight of the slaves, but by the selfish economic interests of capitalism—which requires a free labor market.

This last clause is true. Capitalism cannot work with slave labor. It was the agrarian, feudal South that maintained slavery. It was the industrial, capitalistic North that wiped it out—as capitalism wiped out slavery and serfdom in the whole civilized world of the 19th century.

What greater virtue can one ascribe to a social system than the fact that it leaves no possibility for any man to serve his own interests by enslaving other men? What nobler system could be desired by anyone whose goal is man's well-being?

But that is not the collectivists' goal.

Capitalism has created the highest standard of living ever known on earth. The evidence is incontrovertible. The contrast between West and East Berlin is the latest demonstration, like a laboratory experiment for all to see.

Yet those who are loudest in proclaiming their desire to eliminate poverty are loudest in denouncing capitalism. Man's well-being is not their goal.

The "underdeveloped" nations are an alleged problem to the world. Most of them are destitute. Some, like Brazil, loot (or nationalize) the property of foreign investors; others, like the Congo, slaughter foreigners, including women and children; after which, all of them scream for foreign help, for technicians and money.

It is only the indecency of altruistic doctrines that permits them to hope to get away with it.

If those nations were taught to establish capitalism, with full protection of property rights, their problems would vanish. Men who could afford it would invest private capital in the development of natural resources, expecting to earn profits. They would bring the technicians, the funds, the civilizing influence and the employment which those nations need. Everyone would profit, at no one's expense or sacrifice.

But this would be "selfish" and, therefore, evil—according to the altruists' code.

Instead, they prefer to seize men's earnings—through taxation—and pour them down any foreign drain, and watch our own economic growth slow down year by year.

Next time you refuse yourself some necessity you can't afford or some small luxury which would have made the difference between pleasure and drudgery—ask yourself what part of your money has gone to pay for a crumbling road in Cambodia or for the support of those "selfless" little altruists who play the role of big shots in the jungle, at taxpayers' expense.

If you wish to stop it, you must begin by realizing that altruism is not a doctrine of love, but of hatred for man.

Collectivism does not preach sacrifice as a temporary means to some desirable end. Sacrifice is its end—sacrifice as a way of life. It is man's independence, success, prosperity and happiness that collectivists wish to destroy.

Observe the snarling, hysterical hatred with which they greet any suggestion that sacrifice is not necessary, that a non-sacrificial society is possible to men, that it is the only society able to achieve man's well-being.

If capitalism had never existed, any honest humanitarian should have been struggling to invent it. But when you see men struggling to evade its existence, to misrepresent its nature and to destroy its last remnants—you may be sure that whatever their motives, love for man is not one of them.

The Season of Platitudes

OCTOBER 7, 1962—For the next few weeks there will be no political discussions in America: we have entered the Season of Platitudes—an election campaign.

All issues, principles and definitions vanish during an election campaign. They dissolve into a fog of rubber terms that can mean anything to anyone—while the candidates compete for how to be misunderstood in the greatest number of ways by the greatest number of people.

For instance, here are two statements launching the present campaign:

President Kennedy extolled his party's "record of progress and compassion"—and declared that his opponents had been "deadlocked in divided, divisive, do-nothing government."

Governor Rockefeller, comparing the two parties, declared: "Ours is a clean, clear record of progress, growth and human concern. . . . Theirs is a record of stagnation, obstruction and incompetence."

Ask yourself whether there is any political party anywhere in the world whose program would not fit under declarations of this kind.

Yet this is the only type of statement we are given, to indicate in what direction our candidates intend to lead us.

Any differences among them are only a matter of degree and are chiefly confined to one category: larger or smaller handouts to various pressure groups, such as "Medicare."

It is during a campaign that the clearest thinking and most honest debating are needed. Instead, it is during a campaign that people throw their minds out of focus and go through the motions of ritual, in a daze of hope and bromides.

Who is responsible for it? The voters, when they pretend that they are hearing something. The politicians, when they pretend that the nation has given them a "mandate"—for a program they never discussed.

The greater part of the blame rests on the voters. When people understand political principles and hold clear-cut convictions, they demand the same of their politicians. But in a "mixed economy," it is political principles that are mixed—and no politician dares unmix them.

A politician's first concern is to get elected—without which he cannot achieve his goals, whether they are noble or ignoble, whether he is a crusading idealist or a plain ward-heeler.

If the voters approach elections with nothing better than the desperate feeling that "somebody ought to do something," if they evade or ignore political principles—a politician will follow suit. (Which is why our age is not distinguished by the great stature of its political leaders.)

An election campaign is not the time to teach people the fundamentals of political theory, and a candidate is not a teacher. He can only try to cash in on such ideas as he believes the people to hold. He is not the cause of political trends, he is their product.

Who, then, is the cause? The country's intellectuals.

The study and definition of political theory is a full-time job. Just as all people cannot be automobile manufacturers, but can judge and select which car they wish to buy, so they cannot be political philosophers, but can judge the theories presented to them and form their own convictions accordingly. It is on this crucial responsibility that modern intellectuals have defaulted.

The dreary clowning of today's election campaigns originates in our college classrooms. The evasive mess—a mixture of Marx, Keynes and moral cowardice—taught in most classes of political science, would make our candidates look like paragons of frankness and precision, by comparison.

The people know that something is terribly wrong in today's world and that they are given no choice. But how can they make themselves heard? They are not in the profession of "opinion-making."

They sense, but cannot identify, that the real issue under all the evasions is: capitalism versus socialism. But that is the issue which neither the "liberals" nor the "conservatives" dare face or discuss.

The people are taking the only way out, still open to them: the protest vote. Predominantly, they are voting, not for anything, but against it. The trend in most semi-free countries, notably in England, is to keep voting out whoever is in. It is a temporary means to prevent the entrenchment of a single clique in power.

But those who are concerned with the future should realize that political trends are merely registered, not made, at the polls. And to change today's trends, it is not enough to be merely anti-collectivist.

It can be done only by: (a) acquiring the knowledge of a full, consistent theory of capitalism; (b) communicating it to others; (c) bombarding political representatives, not with emotional appeals, but with intelligent questions aimed at making them specify the meaning of the generalities they offer us.

People should be taught not to accept it when candidates promise the country to sail, without saying where—or promise a New Frontier, without stating of what—or promise "a vigorous leadership," which fearlessly blasts our steel industry, but folds up in Cuba and Berlin.

To change the trend, one must work to create an enlightened electorate. And one must begin by realizing that elections are won in every month of the year—except November.

Our Alleged Competitor

OCTOBER 14,1962—Those who still believe that altruism is moral and collectivism is practical will do well to consider the meaning of the current news from Soviet Russia.

On September 24, the Soviet government announced that it was "postponing" another one of its "five-year plans": the abolition of the income tax. That plan had been proclaimed, with thunderous publicity, in 1960 and had promised to abolish income taxes gradually over a period of five years.

With the same noisy bluff, Khrushchev had announced that the Russians' per capita consumption of meat and butter would surpass the Americans' in a few years. Instead, what the Russian consumers got, last summer, was a 25 percent increase in the prices of meat and butter.

But the Soviet government's expenditures for "the public interest"— for industrial development, space projects and foreign aid—will go on, uncut.

Here is your pure, classic example of general self-sacrifice. This is what the doctrine of "the public interest" means, is and does.

If, forty-five years ago, the altruist-collectivists could claim some excuse for their alleged ideals—for the belief that government planning would abolish poverty, ease the burden of toil and create prosperity for all—what excuse have they now?

In 1917, at the start of the revolution, the Russian standard of living was unspeakably low. The Soviet system brought it still lower. The misery of Soviet existence is incommunicable to Americans. One can merely suggest it by saying that the whole of a man's mental, physical and emotional energy, in Soviet Russia, is devoted to an agonized struggle for his next meal.

But the Soviet rulers assured the people that this was only temporary. They brandished slogans, banners, posters and mass executions, exhorting the people to patience and self-sacrifice for the sake of the country's industrialization. They blamed all hardships on Russia's economic backwardness and on the plotting of foreign imperialists. Industrialization, they promised, would make up for it all, and Soviet progress would surpass the decadent West.

Look through the newspaper files for the forty-five years since. You will find a succession of five-year plans and failures, and bloody purges of scapegoats to account for the failures. The Russian people's standard of living ("standard of dying" would be more accurate) has not changed; shoes, wristwatches, cosmetics are   still luxuries; the production of sufficient food is still an unsolved problem.

Nothing has changed—except the production of public monuments. The starved, ragged Soviet wretches drag themselves now, servicing some giant factories, some hydro-electric dams, a marble-vaulted subway, a hideous skyscraper representing a university, and countless parades in honor of conveniently photogenic young men who return from travels in "outer spaces."

At first, it might have seemed plausible that one should sacrifice oneself (and others) for the sake of helping the poor in one's own country. Now, with the entire country (except the ruling elite) reduced to the lowest level of misery, those same poor, unhelped, are drained by further sacrifices—for the sake of helping the poor of Cuba and Africa.

At first, it might have seemed plausible that the sacrifices were temporary and that industrialization would bring abundance for all.

But industrialization is not a static goal; it is a dynamic process with a rapid rate of obsolescence. So the wretched serfs of a planned economy, who starved while waiting for steam engines and tractors, are now starving while waiting for atomic power and interplanetary travel.

Thus, in a "people's state," the progress of science is a threat to the people, and every advance is taken out of the workers' shrieking hides.

This was not the history of capitalism.

Emerging at the turn of the 19th century, capitalism transformed the world in a few brief decades, creating an unprecedented standard of living for all classes. And with every subsequent decade, with every scientific discovery or technological advance, that standard of living kept rising.

Under capitalism, progress and prosperity were not opposites, but corollaries.

And whenever anyone asks a nation for sacrifices, it is not progress that he will achieve.

America's magnificent achievements—which the Soviets are copying, borrowing and stealing—were not created by public sacrifices, but by the productive genius of free men who pursued their own "selfish" interests and the making of their own private fortunes.

They did not tax you for America's industrial development. They gave you jobs, higher wages and cheaper goods with every new machine they invented, thus raising their productivity and yours—thus moving forward and profiting, not suffering, every step of the way.

Observe that with the growth of statist controls, the rate of our economic growth has been declining. Yet it is capitalism that our political-intellectual leaders regard as "immoral"—and it is socialism that they regard as "practical." (!)

If you saw a drunken bank robber squandering the savings of millions of people on a single champagne-orgy at the Waldorf-Astoria—you would not regard him as economically sound nor as a dangerous threat to a productive industrialist. Yet this precisely is the moral meaning, the economic position and the competitive "threat" of Soviet Russia's alleged technological progress.

Britain's "National Socialism"

OCTOBER 21,1962—The advocates of that political "twilight zone" which is known as "the middle-of-the-road"—who believe that in today's global conflict capitalism and socialism are on the same side, the side of freedom, progress and peace, against a common enemy, communism—have just received an enlightening slap in the face from Mr. Hugh Gaitskell, leader of the British Labor party.

In the sweep of the same gesture, Mr. Gaitskell has torn the last shreds of pretense from the ideological bankruptcy of the modern "liberals."

For decades, the "liberals" have regarded "nationalism" as an arch-evil of capitalism. They denounced national self-interest—they permitted no distinction between intelligent patriotism and blind, racist chauvinism, deliberately lumping them together—they smeared all opponents of internationalist doctrines as "reactionaries," "fascists" or "isolationists"—and they brought this country to the stage where expressions such as "America First" became terms of opprobrium.

They clamored that nationalism was the cause of wars—and that the only way to achieve global peace was to dissolve all national boundaries, sacrifice national sovereignty and merge into the United Nations or into One World.

And suddenly, on October 3—as suddenly and cynically as two leaders of the previous generation announced the Stalin-Hitler pact—Hugh Gaitskell, the socialist, announced that he opposes Britain's entry into the European Common Market, in the name of—nationalism.

The six countries comprising the Common Market are not capitalistic—there are, unfortunately, no capitalistic countries in today's world. They are "mixed economies," but the free, capitalistic element is dominant in their economics, and their foreign policy is anti-communist.

These six countries are Europe's bulwark against Soviet Russia. It is generally known that Russia opposes them and fears their economic success. That success has been spectacular, as the creative power of capitalism—even of semi-capitalism—has always been.

Rising out of the shambles left by dictatorships and war, these semi-capitalistic countries have reached a level of prosperity that shames

56

their semi-socialist neighbors. But their greatest miracle is the cooperation of France and Germany. These two have been mortal enemies for many centuries, like an unhealing wound tearing European history time and bloody time again. An economic system that could transform France and Germany into partners deserves a reverential awe from any honest lover of peace—or, at least, a thoughtful study.

But, at the annual conference of the Labor party, in the gray, drained, shrinking hulk of what had once been a great, free country, Mr. Gaitskell announced that his party opposes Britain's entry into the European Economic Community—except on five conditions which, if accepted, would negate the E.E.C.'s basic concept.

The two significant conditions are: Britain's right to plan her own economy and to pursue her own foreign policy.

The British people "are not prepared to accept supranationalism," Mr. Gaitskell declared—and proceeded to deliver such an avalanche of stale, chauvinistic bromides about the obligation to and preservation of the British Commonwealth that an American newspaper summed it up as: "Labor Party joins Col. Blimp."

While the American people are being urged to surrender their freedom, their rights, their wealth and even their military defense to the mercy of the majority vote of the savage tribes of the whole world—Mr. Gaitskell declared that the British people would not submit to the majority vote of a European federal parliament, if such vote went against them.

"Mr. Gaitskell," wrote the British correspondent of an American paper, "like many in his party and, indeed, many in all parties, is wary of a Europe that might become a tight, anti-socialist, anti-communist bloc."

Such is the purpose and meaning of all the internationalist guff which is destroying America: global peace, international democracy, a World Government and an unlimited majority rule are ideals only so long as the majority votes for socialism; but should an international organization choose to establish a freer system, "the right to plan" a nation's economy takes precedence over all those "ideals," including world peace.

Since the foreign policy of the Common Market is committed to an anti-communist stand, what sort of independent foreign policy does

Mr. Gaitskell seek to pursue? Against whom is his policy to be directed and in whose favor?

Basic principles can neither be ignored nor escaped. In spite of the West's disgraceful evasions, the issue of capitalism versus socialism is coming out into the open. When the chips are down, the socialists find war and communism preferable to prosperity and capitalism.

American "liberals" are now facing a test. Do they have any principles left? Or will they swallow and support Britain's "National Socialism"?

If the Labor party wins the next British election, will we find ourselves maneuvered into helping socialist Britain and communist Russia to destroy the last remnants of semi-capitalist Europe?

The answer will be determined by the foreign policy views of the candidates you are about to elect.

Nationalism vs. Internationalism

NOVEMBER 4,1962—The issue of nationalism versus internationalism—as I pointed out in last week's column—is approaching a climax and requires a clear-cut stand. It is one of the deadliest and least defined of today's issues.

Championed and propagated by "liberals" for many decades, internationalism is collectivism applied to the relationships of nations. Just as domestic collectivism holds that an individual's freedom and interests must be sacrificed to the "public interest" of society—so internationalism holds that a nation's sovereignty and interests must be sacrificed to a global community.

The United States is, perhaps, the only nation that has taken this doctrine seriously and is its greatest victim. Our domestic policy, we are constantly told, must be determined by our foreign policy and subordinated to the requirements of the world situation; international problems come first, domestic problems second.

But the current controversy over Britain's entry into the Common Market has blasted that doctrine, creating an eloquent paradox. "It is the Conservatives, or Tories," wrote an American newspaper, "hitherto the principal exponents of British sovereignty and empire, who are taking Britain into a union with the Continent. And it is the Laborites, the internationally minded Socialists . . . who now lead a charge against making Britain 'a province of Europe.' "

Contrary to all the internationalists, it is domestic policies that are of primary importance, not foreign affairs. A nation's own political system is its first concern. And the basic issue in today's world is not such superficial and artificial questions as nationalism versus internationalism, but capitalism versus socialism.

The basic principle of capitalism is voluntary trade to mutual benefit, among individuals and among nations. The basic principle of socialism is forced self-sacrifice, in both fields.

It is only on the basis of individual rights and interests that the interests of a nation can be defined and protected; it is only on the basis of national interests that any sort of international cooperation can be achieved.

There is a crucial difference between joining a semi-capitalistic type of international organization, such as the Common Market—or an altruist-collectivist type, such as the United Nations.

Observe that the U.N. is achieving the opposite of its alleged goals. It demanded the sacrifice of national interests; instead, it has led to the worst kind of primordial nationalism: to tribal racism.

The Common Market cannot be said fully to represent capitalistic principles. It is a "mixed economy" whose policies are pro-capitalistic, not explicitly, but implicitly and by default—just as the United States, at present, is a "mixed economy" moving toward socialism, not explicitly, but implicitly and by default.

The Common Market is a precarious structure guided, not by firm political principles, but by the expediency of the moment. Starting from war-time ruins, it turned to freedom, not as a philosophy, but as an expedient, and adopted one aspect of capitalism: free trade. The results were miraculous.

The position of capitalism in the Common Market today is that of socialism in the semi-free economies of the 19th century: a principle smuggled into an economy and left unidentified. Socialism was not accepted by the world as a consciously chosen program or system; it won gradually, in single steps urged by the intellectuals and adopted by the pragmatic, range-of-the-moment policy of governments that refused to consider the consequences of their actions.

Every government control imposed on a nation's economy created problems that required further controls that required still further controls, and so on. It is by such steps that a prosperous world was brought to the misery of socialized bankruptcy.

A similar process, in reverse, now confronts the Common Market. One liberated area of economic activity interferes with government planning and requires the liberation of further areas that require the liberation of still further areas, and so on. (This is the reason why the Common Market cannot include a socialist Britain.) If the Common Market is to retain its achievements, that is the process it will have to follow.

Whether it will, depends on the theoretical perceptiveness and courage of its leaders. Long-range destruction can be achieved by blind, short-range pragmatism; long-range success, cannot.

A growing prosperity will bring growing demands for unearned benefits by statist pressure-groups; if they are not resisted, they will undercut the Common Market and wreck it. But they can be resisted only by the political philosophy of laissez-faire capitalism, explicitly adopted and upheld.

How much destruction will the world have to endure before men realize this?

The politicians of the Western world are clinging desperately to the collapsing status quo—to the fiction of a workable "mixed economy"—dreading the necessity to identify the issue. The future depends on the emergence of statesmen who will challenge socialism not by silent expediency, but by proudly open conviction.

The Cuban Crisis

NOVEMBER 11,1962—As of this writing, the Cuban crisis is a question mark suspended in fog.

The stand taken by President Kennedy may have two opposite meanings. If we maintain an uncompromising policy, it may mean a historical turning point: the return of the United States to dignity, efficacy and national self-esteem—and, consequently, the eventual return of the world to a civilized state of existence. If we soften and compromise, it will mean the lowest surrender in our disastrous foreign policy of the last thirty years.

There are disturbing signs, pointing toward the second possibility.

The first few days of the crisis were a dramatic demonstration of a fact forgotten by today's ideologists: the fact that right is might. Although Mr. Kennedy's declaration of October 22 left much to be desired, the mere fact that an American president asserted this country's rightful self-interest in an uncompromising manner was like a sunburst in the gray murk of a world where the right had been retreating apologetically for thirty shameful years.

The results of that declaration were an eloquent proof of what the more perceptive of us had been saying for years: that Soviet Russia's alleged power is a gigantic bluff, built up by the concessions of her adversaries—that Russia, like Nazi Germany, like any bully, feeds on appeasement and will retreat placatingly at the first sound of firm opposition.

The countries of Latin America—that had been hedging and hampering us in most international issues, including the issue of Cuba, so long as we courted them, seeking their approval—joined us instantly and unanimously when we took an independent stand. Those countries were not fully to blame for their former attitude: nobody can trust an international Caspar Milquetoast.

With the same eagerly immediate response, Western Europe and all the semi-free nations of the world rallied to our support, in a great wave of popular feeling, as if we were the long-sought leader of the world and its last hope—as, for a few brief days, we were. Observe that this response—which none of our altruistic global schemes had ever been able to arouse—was aroused by our determination to uphold our own rights.

"It's about time!" was the cry of the American people, greeting our new policy. That cry showed the enormous miscalculation into which Soviet Russia and her sympathizers had poured billions' worth of scare propaganda. It showed the difference between human beings and those who'd rather be Red than dead, having never been alive.

In those first few days, people would have followed Mr. Kennedy, forgetting their doubts. They will not follow him now.

After winning Khrushchev's compliance with his conditions, Mr. Kennedy negated the moral base of his own stand—the principle that the security of the United States is not subject to negotiations—and turned his victory over to the amoral bargaining of the U.N., where the claims of aggressors and victims are "neutrally" regarded as equal.

What followed was the hypocritical futility of the U.N. routine and a series of moral compromises on our part—such as the proposed selection of "neutral" observers to supervise the dismantling of Cuba's missile bases. By what stretch of what rubber standard was our national security to be delivered into the power of such countries as: Brazil, Mexico, Ethiopia, Burma, Nigeria and socialist Sweden? Was this the proper policy of a great sovereign nation?

During U Thant's futile visit to Cuba, we suspended our naval blockade and our air surveillance—as a gesture of "good will." Good will—toward whom? Toward Castro and Khrushchev?

If, on seeing a policeman, a thug turns away from a house he had intended to dynamite, the appropriate thing for the policeman to say is: "Don't let me catch you at it again." It is not appropriate to send messages of good will, hailing the thug as a protector of law and order.

The solemn sternness of our stand has been undercut. It does not matter now what form the grotesque contortions of the U.N. will take and whether our security will ultimately be entrusted to Burma, to Switzerland, to the Red Cross or to the Boy Scouts.

What matters is the ominous questions which this performance raises. Why was the building of the Cuban missile bases allowed to go as far as it did? What was the matter with our intelligence service? Why did Mr. Kennedy's declaration come so late? Is the U.N. performance being staged to save Khrushchev's face—or to confuse and exhaust the American people?

There is too much talk in official and semi-official circles about a conciliatory policy toward Khrushchev and the necessity of making "some" concessions. Will we surrender Guantanamo base, or Berlin, or Turkey—and will this be presented to us, in a trumpet-blare of platitudes, as a victory that saved us from nuclear war?

It is too soon to tell. But one thing is certain: if Mr. Kennedy makes any concessions as a result of the Cuban crisis, it will be an open invitation to further crises and outrages—a proof given to an international criminal that crime does pay.

If a burglar made repeated attempts to rob your safe and failed, but was given a ten-dollar bill each time, to compensate him for his effort—what would be the ultimate fate of your possessions and who would be responsible for it?

If any pressure group is attempting such a policy, the only thing we can do at present is to let the Administration know that we understand what kind of game is being played.

Post-Mortem, 1962

NOVEMBER 18,1962—In the past decades, our elections have taken the following pattern: (1) during the campaign, both parties offer nothing but a package-deal of stale generalities, which can mean all things to all men, evading any discussion of basic principles or issues; (2) after the election, commentators and party leaders declare which basic principles and issues the people have endorsed.

This year, the dispirited grayness of our political atmosphere has thickened. The commentators are nervously cautious. Both parties claim victory in a perfunctory manner, offering tired rationalizations to support their claims.

The truth is that there were no victories, since no goals or programs were at stake. Both parties lost—and, in most cases, the formal victories are not an indication of who the voters were for, but only of which particular candidate they were more strongly against.

The United States, at present, is a country without political ideology, without any intellectual movement, without direction or goal. We are paralyzed by the unadmitted knowledge that we are trapped in the crumbling structure of a "mixed economy"—and, while the girders are cracking under our feet, about to collapse, our political leaders are haggling over which rugs and drapes to loot from some rooms for the decoration of others.

The issue which neither camp dares identify is the fact that a "mixed economy" is an unstable, untenable mixture of capitalism and socialism. Most Democrats do not want to establish socialism; most Republicans do not want to advocate capitalism. So both are reduced, by default, to the lowest of all common denominators: to the position of "well-meaning statists," which is a contradiction in terms.

There was only one political program offered to the voters: the status quo—and only two kinds of leadership: those who wish to leap or those who wish to crawl into the same abyss.

Nothing can be learned from such an election about the political views of the people. But certain observations can be made.

It is not the people, but their alleged leaders who are guilty of apathy. The people turned out in unusually large numbers, but were offered no unequivocal way to register their views.

The ticket-splitting, the crossing of party lines, the upsets, the unexpected reversals of predictions seem to indicate that the people were groping for an ideological consistency which was not to be found. Party labels mean nothing any longer. Nobody is fooled by the pretense that a vote for a Republican such as Governor Rockefeller is a vote for "conservatism," while a vote for a Democrat such as Senator Lausche of Ohio is a vote for "liberalism."

It is significant that on the Federal level most incumbents were reelected, in spite of President Kennedy's attacks on Congress. On the state level, where twelve governorships changed hands, the protest-voting was obvious: the protest was directed against whichever party happened to be in power.

It is significant that so many contests were won by such narrow margins. The country is as divided as it was in 1960—and it is futile, or worse, to pretend that President Kennedy has gained in popularity.

If a vote for the Democratic party means a vote for the New Frontier, then it is significant that the Democrats won in such states as Connecticut and Massachusetts, with a large population of suburban "intellectuals," but lost in such industrial states as Ohio, Michigan and Pennsylvania. It supports the claim that welfare statism is a product of suburbia and not of the industrial "proletariat."

Perhaps the least excusable attitude is that of many Republicans who assert dejectedly that the people should have voted against Mr. Kennedy's record—even though no real criticism of that record had been voiced by Republican leaders. A party that expects the people to take the stand it lacks the courage to take does not deserve a position of leadership.

The most grotesque touch of the campaign was provided by the post-election comment of D.H. Jaquith, the gubernatorial candidate of a so-called "Conservative Party" in New York state. According to *The New York Times*, Mr. Jaquith "regards himself as a 'middle-of-the-roader' rather than a rightist" and is quoted as saying: "I don't see any middle-of-the-roaders. Democracy is destroying itself when those who promise the most are elected."

If Mr. Jaquith did not see any middle-of-the-roaders in this election, one must wonder at what it was that he did see.

And if such is the vision of men who posture as capitalism's or America's defenders, let no one say that capitalism was rejected or defeated by the blindness of the people.

How To Demoralize a Nation

NOVEMBER 25, 1962—Among the many baffling aspects of our policy on the Cuban crisis to date, the most demoralizing one was a gratuitous little event of grave psychological consequences: the fact that on November 13 President Kennedy attended a performance of the Soviet Bolshoi Ballet.

The Cuban crisis is not over. The conditions laid down in Mr. Kennedy's declaration of October 22 have not been met; Khrushchev has double-crossed us, as usual; as far as any objective knowledge, evidence or proof is concerned, nuclear missiles are still in Cuba, waiting to be dropped on us from jet bombers. Is this the proper time for the President of the United States to attend the Soviet ballet?

On October 22, Mr. Kennedy declared, properly, that the Soviet military build-up in Cuba was an intolerable threat to our national security and that we would take any step necessary to eliminate it. In the days that followed, the American people faced the possibility of a nuclear war breaking out at any moment (if the assertions of our political leaders of the past decade are to be trusted). The people faced it magnificently; they were ready and eager; they believed that our country was in deadly danger and they responded like men.

Consider what courage was required of the men in our armed services—of the Marine Corps, the Navy, the Air Force, summoned to converge on the Caribbean—and of their families. Consider what solemn dedication and quiet heroism they displayed. The situation has not changed; they are still at their posts, under threat of the enemy's nuclear fire. What are they to feel—what are they expected to feel—when they hear that the President is spending an evening at the enemy's ballet? Shouldn't Mr. Kennedy have abstained from it, out of respect for them, if for no other reason?

It is impossible to believe that a President would have so cynical a contempt for the sensibility of the American people that he would consciously ignore the implications of his "fraternizing" gesture. It is not much easier to believe that he could be unconscious of them.

What are we to think of the course of our policy in the past two weeks? The Cuban crisis has all but vanished in the quicksands of the U.N.—and if we judge by the queer bubbles popping up on the surface, some fantastic game is being played. The question is: by whom and at whose expense?

Surely our Navy's "inspection" of covered crates on the decks of Soviet ships is not intended to be taken as a substitute for on-site inspection, or to be taken seriously at all. For whose benefit is our Navy going through so gruesomely farcical a pretense?

We are told that diplomacy is a delicate process and that Mr. Kennedy must be tactful, but firm. We are also told that the danger of a nuclear war lies in the possibility that Khrushchev will miscalculate and push things too far, considering us too soft to fight. Was Mr. Kennedy's attendance at the ballet a sign of firmness, severity and determination?

Mr. Kennedy did more than attend the ballet: he went backstage to compliment the dancers, with Soviet Ambassador Dobrynin acting as his interpreter and with all American newsmen barred. Arthur Krock commented on November 15: "If all the American reporters who wanted to accompany the President backstage had been admitted, the personal compliment of his visit would have been diminished. But no member of the White House staff thought of the usual solution of having the reporters choose one of their number to attend the little ceremony. However, the representative of Tass was admitted because, as it was later and inadequately explained, he is 'after all, an employee of the Russian Government.' "

No one can pretend that this was an issue of "art" and not a diplomatic issue. The question of art is not applicable to any Soviet importation: there is no such thing as free art in Russia, there is only state art. Therefore, regardless of the imports' merits or demerits, it is not the "artists" but the Soviet government that one sanctions and supports when one attends a Soviet ballet or concert or movie.

Is it proper for the President of the United States to act as a Soviet stage-door Johnnie?

In the past decade, we have been asked by all our political leaders—and particularly by Mr. Kennedy—to make unlimited sacrifices to save our country, because we are engaged in a cold war with a deadly enemy. We have also been told repeatedly that the issue of morale is crucially important during a war, be it a cold war or a hot one.

What will Mr. Kennedy's gesture do to our morale? Will it inspire us to make sacrifices? Will it give us confidence in our leaders and their policies? Will it prompt us to take the crisis (or anything) seriously?

Is that the way to lead a world crusade—or to breed cynical apathy?

The next time sociological observers ponder over the causes of our cultural disintegration, of the bitter lethargy, the hopeless cynicism, the hysterical aimlessness, the stagnant fear, the collapse of moral standards and moral values, particularly among the young—let them take note.

Freedom of Speech

DECEMBER 2,1962—The statists' policy of creating intellectual chaos by perverting all moral and political principles was eloquently illustrated in the disgraceful issue of Alger Hiss' appearance on an ABC television program on November 11.

That a man convicted of perjury in the matter of being a Soviet spy should be invited to pass judgment on a former Vice President of the United States, is a national disgrace. It is typical of the hooligan extremes to which certain "liberals" permit themselves to go—and it can be stopped only by the moral protest of all civilized persons.

But what became ominously clear, in the aftermath of that event, is the means by which the statists intend to disarm such protests and, in effect, to silence the last echoes of morality in our bankrupt culture. They intend to destroy freedom of speech—by invoking "freedom of speech."

Without touching upon whatever contractual agreements existed between the sponsors of that program, the network and Howard K. Smith, the basic principle to consider is: do sponsors have the right to choose what they wish to support or does a man lose the right to his own convictions by becoming a TV sponsor?

This question was injected into the issue by Mr. Smith's defenders who—unable to answer the unanswerable moral charges—chose to cry that any protest from a sponsor constitutes "censorship."

Freedom of speech means: freedom from suppression, interference or punitive action by the government—and nothing else. It does not pertain to a man's relations with private individuals, only to his relations with the government; it forbids the government to silence a man in the expression of his views.

No private agency can silence a man—because no private individual or group has the legal power to use physical force against other individuals or groups and to compel them to act against their own voluntary choice. Only a government holds that power.

The same is true of censorship. No private agency can suppress a publication; only the government can.

When private individuals disagree with an idea, all they can do is refuse to listen or refuse to aid, abet, finance or support it in any way—which is their inalienable right.

The right of free speech does not mean that others must provide a man with a printing press, a publishing house, a newspaper, a theater or a television studio through which to express his views. It means that others may not use force to stop him or those who agree with him from earning such facilities by their own efforts through the normal processes of free trade.

But the statists are struggling to spread the idea that a "right" includes its material implementation—that the right of "free speech" includes a right to demand the financial support of others, whether they agree with one's views or not—and that a private individual's refusal to finance an opponent constitutes a violation of the opponent's "rights."

This means that the ability to provide the material tools for the expression of ideas deprives a man of the right to hold any ideas. It means that a publisher has to publish books he considers worthless, false or evil—and that a TV sponsor has to finance commentators who choose to affront his convictions and to disgrace him in the hearing of the whole nation. It means that one group of men acquires the "right" to unlimited license—while another group is reduced to helpless irresponsibility.

Would anything resembling freedom, justice, rights or morality be possible under a set-up of that kind?

No private action is "censorship" nor infringement of "free speech." The right to act on one's own convictions is the prerequisite of a man of integrity—and this includes the right not to support one's own enemies. Every man is free to advocate his views, but he must bear the responsibility for them and the consequences, including disagreement with others, opposition and unpopularity.

It is precisely the rights of unpopular minorities, of non-conformists or innovators that the political concept of "free speech" is designed to protect. Its function is to protect dissenters from forcible suppression—not to guarantee them the support, advantages or rewards of a popularity they have not earned.

The constitutional guarantee of free speech reads: "Congress shall make no law . . . abridging the freedom of speech, or of the press. . . ." It does not demand that private citizens provide a microphone for the man who advocates their destruction, or a passkey for the burglar who wants to seize their property, or a knife for the murderer who intends to cut their throats.

The Munich of World War III?

DECEMBER 9,1962 — "Neither the United States of America nor the world community of nations can tolerate deliberate deception and offensive threats on the part of any nation, large or small," said President Kennedy on October 22.

He quoted the Soviet government's statements that no offensive weapons had been sent to Cuba—and he solemnly declared that those statements were false.

Enumerating the steps necessary to defend our security, he said: "Our resolution will call for the prompt dismantling and withdrawal of all offensive weapons in Cuba under the supervision of U.N. observers before the quarantine can be lifted."

On November 20, in his news conference, Mr. Kennedy declared: "I have today been informed by Chairman Khrushchev that all of the IL-28 bombers now in Cuba will be withdrawn in thirty days. . . . I have this afternoon instructed the Secretary of Defense to lift our naval quarantine."

Why? What had happened to make Mr. Kennedy retreat and accept, as a guarantee of our national security, the word of a man he had branded as a liar just one month earlier?

During that month, Khrushchev had double-crossed us again. The conditions laid down by Mr. Kennedy have not been met. The promise of on-site inspections has been broken. The only public evidence of the dismantling of Cuban bases was provided by our own aerial photographs. As to nuclear missiles—as far as objective knowledge, evidence or proof is concerned— they may still be in Cuba and may be dropped on us from jet bombers.

Since no inspections were arranged, yet our quarantine was lifted, how can we know whether all the bombers will be removed or whether the thirty-day period will be used to bring more weapons to Cuba, as secretly as they were brought before? What assurance do we have? None but Khrushchev's word.

The Cuban crisis is not over. It has merely been sidetracked to vanish in the quicksands of the U.N.—and if we judge by the queer bubbles popping up on the surface, some fantastic game is being played. The question is: by whom and at whose expense?

72

Surely our Navy's "inspection" of covered crates on the decks of Soviet ships was not intended to be taken as a substitute for on-site inspection, or to be taken seriously at all. For whose benefit did our Navy go through so gruesomely farcical a pretense?

Apparently, it was for the benefit of the American people—because, in his news conference of November 20, Mr. Kennedy declared: "And our inspection at sea of these departing ships has confirmed that the number of missiles reported by the Soviet Union as having been brought into Cuba, which closely corresponded to our own information, has now been removed."

It is hard to say which of the two possibilities is worse: that Mr. Kennedy has that low an estimate of the American people's intelligence—or that his own credulity stretches that far.

If he had other sources of information, why insult the public by any reference to that "inspection at sea"? If he had no other sources, is this what our Commander-in-Chief accepts as military evidence?

On October 22, Mr. Kennedy declared that the Communist military build-up in Cuba "cannot be accepted by this country if our courage and our commitments are ever to be trusted again, by either friend or foe."

How are they to be trusted now? After the free world had rallied unanimously and enthusiastically to support Mr. Kennedy's stand, it saw his gradual and, apparently, causeless retreat. It saw Mr. Kennedy surrender our right to demand objective proof of our security.

If we assume that Mr. Kennedy's demands were met at least to some extent, that Cuba has been partially disarmed, and that this was a symbolic victory for the United States, since it forced Russia to back down and to pretend compliance—why are Mr. Kennedy's advisers working so hard to minimize even that slender gain?

"We have cautioned our friends from drawing too many conclusions from the Cuban experience. The Soviet Union remains a great power." No, this was not said by Mikoyan. It was said by Secretary Rusk.

In reward for his failure to arrange on-site inspections, U Thant has been elected Secretary General of the U.N. Discussing his policy, he declared that international crises should be solved "on the basis of compromise and the principle of give and take on both sides."

Compromise—between aggressors and victims? The "giving" of concessions in exchange for the withdrawal of threats? An international game of nuclear blackmail?

We do not know what goals, ambitions or motives rule the U.N. It is likely that we will not know—until the next Soviet outrage—what purpose the Cuban crisis has been made to serve. We can only watch—and hope that the U.N. clique has not turned the Cuban crisis into the Munich of World War III.

Vandalism

DECEMBER 16,1962—The Vandals were a barbarian tribe who sacked Rome in the 5th century A.D., distinguishing themselves by the blind savagery of their attack on a special kind of victim: works of art. They left behind them a trail of wantonly marred, disfigured, shattered monuments—and an intangible monument of their own: a new concept in the language of civilized men.

"Vandalism," according to the dictionary, is the "willful or ignorant destruction of artistic or literary treasures."

An act of vandalism was televised by NBC on December 6; the victim was Rostand's *Cyrano de Bergerac*.

Artistic ineptitude, as such, is of no significance; but the particular kind of ineptitude displayed by this show is profoundly significant as a gauge of the distance our culture has traveled in its descent to neo-barbarism.

Cyrano de Bergerac is a hymn to man's integrity, independence and self-esteem—a magnificent view of man's heroic spirit that remains untouched by suffering and tragedy. That such a view is alien to modern culture, is obvious; that today's "artists" could not project such values successfully, would not be astonishing. But the almost frightening aspect of that show was the fact that its perpetrators were unable even to recognize those values—as if, to them, the concept of self-esteem were inconceivable.

Their "modern" version presented Cyrano as a beatnik: as an unkempt, self-pitying neurotic with an inferiority complex, who "compensated" for the shape of his nose by belligerent insolence, cheap clowning and abject whining.

In Rostand's play, Cyrano's joyously brilliant humor is the expression of a man who enjoys his own intellectual virtuosity and makes life colorful wherever he goes, whatever he does, for life's sake and his own. In Christopher Plummer's performance, an undignified buffoon kept playing to the gallery, simultaneously spitting at people and pleading to be noticed.

Instead of Rostand's hero whose soul would never surrender to tragedy, Mr. Plummer's creature whined tearfully in a cracked, simpering, senile voice, pleading for pity. The numerous close-ups showed a face that seemed unconscious of the meaning of the sounds it was reciting, with unfocused eyes, trembling jaws and odd, munching lip movements that suggested uncomfortable dentures.

Instead of Rostand's triumphantly proud celebration of integrity in the famous "No, thank you" speech, Mr. Plummer hissed his way through the speech with a venomous malice, projecting an embittered weakling's hatred for the whole universe.

This was the key to the astronomical distance between Rostand and the psychology of the "moderns": wherever Rostand intended magnanimity, it was replaced by malice.

Instead of magnanimity, it was a malicious bluff that Cyrano projected when he acted as Christian's protector. Instead of magnanimity, it was a malicious resentment of Cyrano that Christian projected when he demanded that Roxanne be told the truth. As to Roxanne, instead of a romantic woman who seeks spiritual beauty and grandeur, there fluttered a capricious little chorus girl on a date in an ice-cream parlor, who pouted whenever her boy friends disobeyed her whims.

The script was a butchered remnant of the play, slashed at random, with no greater knowledge than a vandal's of why *Cyrano de Bergerac* is not to be condensed. The direction would have been embarrassing in a high school amateur production. The entire cast mouthed brilliant lines as if they were inarticulate grunts—and it was hard to tell whether this was the "Method" or just plain madness.

In his preface to the Brian Hooker translation of *Cyrano de Bergerac*, Clayton Hamilton wrote, in 1923, that he persuaded Walter Hampden to revive "the most intoxicating play of modern times" by saying: "I want to see Cyrano again; but I am thinking also of the thousands of younger people who have never seen it at all. Won't you give them a chance?"

I am thinking of the millions of younger people who saw its televised corpse. In this day and age, when we hear so much about television's educational duty, I wonder about the ethical standards of those who, depriving the younger people of any knowledge of Romantic art, palm off on them that maudlin piece of neurotic pretentiousness and rob them of the incentive to discover the most uplifting experience the theater has ever had to offer.

There is a state of cultural-esthetic disintegration lower than the modern intellectuals' worship of human depravity and their antagonism to Romantic literature with its projection of man's intellect, integrity, heroism, self-esteem. There is a state lower than that of men who prefer Tennessee Williams to Edmond Rostand: the state of those who see no difference between them.

Other
Writings

Textbook of Americanism

This article originally appeared in 1946 in The Vigil, *a publication of The Motion Picture Alliance for the Preservation of American Ideals, Beverly Hills, California. The subject was limited to the sphere of politics, for the purpose of defining and clarifying the basic principles involved in political issues. The twelve questions reprinted here are the first third of a longer project, which was never completed.*

1. What Is the Basic Issue in the World Today?

The basic issue in the world today is between two principles: Individualism and Collectivism.

Individualism holds that man has inalienable rights which cannot be taken away from him by any other man, nor by any number, group or collective of other men. Therefore, each man exists by his own right and for his own sake, not for the sake of the group.

Collectivism holds that man has no rights; that his work, his body and his personality belong to the group; that the group can do with him as it pleases, in any manner it pleases, for the sake of whatever it decides to be its own welfare. Therefore, each man exists only by the permission of the group and for the sake of the group.

These two principles are the roots of two opposite social systems. The basic issue of the world today is between these two systems.

2. What Is a Social System?

A social system is a code of laws which men observe in order to live together. Such a code must have a basic principle, a starting point, or it cannot be devised. The starting point is the question: *Is the power of society limited or unlimited?*

Individualism answers: The power of society is limited by the inalienable, individual rights of man. Society may make only such laws as do not violate these rights.

Collectivism answers: The power of society is unlimited. Society may make any laws it wishes, and force them upon anyone in any manner it wishes.

Example: Under a system of *Individualism*, a million men cannot

81

pass a law to kill one man for their own benefit. If they go ahead and kill him, they are breaking the law—which protects his right to life—and they are punished.

Under a system of *Collectivism*, a million men (or anyone claiming to represent them) can pass a law to kill one man (or any minority), whenever they think they would benefit by his death. His right to live is not recognized.

Under Individualism, it is illegal to kill the man and it is legal for him to protect himself. The law is on the side of a *right*. Under Collectivism, it is legal for the majority to kill a man and it is illegal for him to defend himself. The law is on the side of a *number*.

In the first case, the law represents a moral principle.

In the second case, the law represents the idea that there are no moral principles, and men can do anything they please, provided there's enough of them.

Under a system of Individualism, men are equal before the law at all times. Each has the same rights, whether he is alone or has a million others with him.

Under a system of Collectivism, men have to gang up on one another—and whoever has the biggest gang at the moment, holds *all* rights, while the loser (the individual or the minority) has *none*. Any man can be an absolute master or a helpless slave—according to the size of his gang.

An example of the first system: *The United States of America*. (See: The Declaration of Independence.)

An example of the second system: *Soviet Russia* and *Nazi Germany*.

Under the Soviet system, millions of peasants or "kulaks" were exterminated by law, a law justified by the pretext that this was for the benefit of the majority, which the ruling group contended was anti-kulak. Under the Nazi system, millions of Jews were exterminated by law, a law justified by the pretext that this was for the benefit of the majority, which the ruling group contended was anti-Semitic.

The Soviet law and the Nazi law were the unavoidable and consistent result of the principle of Collectivism. When applied in practice, a principle which recognizes no morality and no individual rights, can result in nothing except brutality.

Keep this in mind when you try to decide what is the proper social system. You have to start by answering the first question. *Either the power of society is limited, or it is not.* It can't be both.

3. What Is the Basic Principle of America?

The basic principle of the United States of America is Individualism.

America is built on the principle that Man possesses Inalienable Rights;

• that these rights belong to each *man* as an individual—not to "men" as a group or collective;

• that these rights are the unconditional, private, personal, individual possession of each man—not the public, social, collective possession of a group;

• that these rights are granted to man by the fact of his birth as a man—not by an act of society;

• that man holds these rights, not *from* the Collective nor *for* the Collective, but *against* the Collective—as a barrier which the Collective cannot cross;

• that these rights are man's protection against all other men;

• that only on the basis of these rights can men have a society of freedom, justice, human dignity and decency.

The Constitution of the United States of America is not a document that limits the rights of man—but a document that limits the power of society over man.

4. What Is a Right?

A right is the sanction of independent action. A right is that which can be exercised without anyone's permission.

If you exist only because society permits you to exist—you have no *right* to your own life. A permission can be revoked at any time.

If, before undertaking some action, you must obtain the permission of society—you are not free, whether such permission is granted to you or not. Only a slave acts on permission. A permission is not a right.

Do not make the mistake, at this point, of thinking that a worker is a slave and that he holds his job by his employer's permission. He does not hold it by permission—but *by contract*, that is, by a voluntary mutual agreement. A worker can quit his job. A slave cannot.

5. What Are the Inalienable Rights of Man?

The inalienable Rights of Men are: Life, Liberty and the Pursuit of Happiness.

The Right of Life means that Man cannot be deprived of his life for the benefit of another man nor of any number of other men.

The Right of Liberty means Man's right to individual action, individual choice, individual initiative and individual property. Without the right to private property no independent action is possible.

The Right to the Pursuit of Happiness means man's right to live for himself, to choose what constitutes his own private, personal, individual happiness and to work for its achievement, so long as he respects the same right in others. It means that Man cannot be forced to devote his life to the happiness of another man nor of any number of other men. It means that the collective cannot decide what is to be the purpose of a man's existence nor prescribe his choice of happiness.

6. How Do We Recognize One Another's Rights?

Since Man has inalienable individual rights, this means that the same rights are held, individually, by every man, by all men, at all times. Therefore, the rights of one man cannot and must not violate the rights of another.

For instance: a man has the right to live, but he has no right to take the life of another. He has the right to be free, but no right to enslave another. He has the right to choose his own happiness, but no right to decide that his happiness lies in the misery (or murder or robbery or enslavement) of another. The very right upon which he acts defines the same right of another man, and serves as a guide to tell him what he may or may not do.

Do not make the mistake of the ignorant who think that an individualist is a man who says: "I'll do as I please at everybody else's expense." An individualist is a man who recognizes the inalienable individual rights of man—his own and those of others.

An individualist is a man who says: "I will not run anyone's life— nor let anyone run mine. I will not rule nor be ruled. I will not be a master nor a slave. I will not sacrifice myself to anyone—nor sacrifice anyone to myself."

A collectivist is a man who says: "Let's get together, boys—and then anything goes!"

7. How Do We Determine That a Right Has Been Violated?

A right cannot be violated except by physical force. One man cannot deprive another of his life, nor enslave him, nor forbid him to pursue his happiness, except by using force against him. Whenever a man is made to act without his own free, personal, individual, *voluntary* consent—his right has been violated.

Therefore, we can draw a clear-cut division between the rights of one man and those of another. It is an *objective* division—not subject to differences of opinion, nor to majority decision, nor to the arbitrary decree of society. **No man has the right to initiate the use of physical force against another man.**

The practical rule of conduct in a free society, a society of Individualism, is simple and clear-cut: you cannot expect or demand any action from another man, except through his free, voluntary consent.

Do not be misled on this point by an old collectivist trick which goes like this: There is no absolute freedom anyway, since you are not free to murder; society limits your freedom when it does not permit you to kill; therefore, society holds the right to limit your freedom in any manner it sees fit; therefore, drop the delusion of freedom—freedom is whatever society decides it is.

It is *not* society, nor any social right, that forbids you to kill—but the inalienable *individual* right of another man to live. This is not a "compromise" between two rights—but a line of division that preserves both rights untouched. The division is not derived from an edict of society—but from your own inalienable individual right. The definition of this limit is not set arbitrarily by society—but is implicit in the definition of your own right.

Within the sphere of your own rights, your freedom *is* absolute.

8. What Is the Proper Function of Government?

The proper function of government is to protect the individual rights of man; this means—to protect man against brute force.

In a proper social system, men do not use force against one another; force may be used only in self-defense, that is, in defense of a right violated by force. Men delegate to the government the power to use force in retaliation—and *only* in retaliation.

The proper kind of government *does not* initiate the use of force. It uses force *only* to answer those who have initiated its use. For example: when the government arrests a criminal, it is not the government that violates a right; it is the criminal who has violated a right and by doing so has placed himself outside the principle of rights, where men can have no recourse against him except through force.

Now it is important to remember that all actions defined as criminal in a free society are actions involving force—and only such actions are answered by force.

Do not be misled by sloppy expressions such as "A murderer commits a crime against society." It is not society that a murderer murders, but an individual man. It is not a social right that he breaks, but an individual right. He is not punished for hurting a collective—he has not hurt a whole collective—he has hurt one man. If a criminal robs ten men—it is still not "society" that he has robbed, but ten individuals. There are no "crimes against society'—all crimes are committed against specific men, against individuals. And it is precisely the duty of a proper social system and of a proper government to protect an individual against criminal attack—against force.

When, however, a government becomes an *initiator of force*—the injustice and moral corruption involved are truly unspeakable.

For example: When a Collectivist government orders a man to work and attaches him to a job, under penalty of death or imprisonment—it is the government that initiates the use of force. The man has done no violence to anyone—but the government uses violence against him. There is no possible justification for such a procedure in theory. And there is no possible result in practice—except the blood and the terror which you can observe in any Collectivist country.

The moral perversion involved is this: If men had no government and no social system of any kind, they might have to exist through sheer force and fight one another in any disagreement; in such a state, one man would have a fair chance against one other man; but he would have no chance against ten others. It is not against *an individual* that a man needs protection—but *against a group*. Still, in such a state of anarchy, while any majority gang would have its way, a minority could fight them by any means available. And the gang could not make its rule last.

Collectivism goes a step below savage anarchy: it takes away from man even the chance to fight back. It makes violence legal—and resistance to it illegal. It gives the sanction of law to the organized brute force of a majority (or of anyone who claims to represent it)—and turns the minority into a helpless, disarmed object of extermination. If you can think of a more vicious perversion of justice—name it.

In actual practice, when a Collectivist society violates the rights of a minority (or of one single man), the result is that the majority loses its rights as well, and finds itself delivered into the total power of a small group that rules through sheer brute force.

If you want to understand and keep clearly in mind the difference between the use of force as retaliation (as it is used by the government of an Individualist society) and the use of force as primary policy (as it is used by the government of a Collectivist society), here is the simplest example of it: it is the same difference as that between a murderer and a man who kills in self-defense. The proper kind of government acts on the principle of man's self-defense. A Collectivist government acts like a murderer.

9. Can There Be A "Mixed" Social System?

There can be no social system which is a mixture of Individualism and Collectivism. Either individual rights are recognized in a society, or they are not recognized. They cannot be half-recognized.

What frequently happens, however, is that a society based on Individualism does not have the courage, integrity and intelligence to observe its own principle consistently in every practical application. Through ignorance, cowardice or mental sloppiness, such a society passes laws and accepts regulations which contradict its basic principle and violate the rights of man. To the extent of such violations, society perpetrates injustices, evils and abuses. If the breaches are not corrected, society collapses into the chaos of Collectivism.

When you see a society that recognizes man's rights in some of its laws, but not in others—do not hail it as a "mixed" system and do not conclude that a compromise between basic principles, opposed in theory, can be made to work in practice. Such a society is not working—it is merely disintegrating. Disintegration takes time. Nothing falls to pieces immediateiy—neither a human body nor a human society.

10. Can A Society Exist Without A Moral Principle?

A great many people today hold the childish notion that society can do anything it pleases; that principles are unnecessary, rights are only an illusion, and *expediency* is the practical guide to action.

It is true that society *can* abandon moral principles and turn itself into a herd running amuck to destruction. Just as it is true that a man *can* cut his own throat any time he chooses. But a man *cannot* do this if he wishes to survive. And society *cannot* abandon moral principles if it expects to exist.

Society is a large number of men who live together in the same country, and who deal with one another. Unless there is a defined, objective moral code, which men understand and observe, they have no way of dealing with one another—since none can know what to expect from his neighbor. The man who recognizes no morality is the criminal; you can do nothing when dealing with a criminal, except try to crack his skull before he cracks yours; you have no other language, no terms of behavior mutually accepted. To speak of a society without moral principles is to advocate that men live together like criminals.

We are still observing, by tradition, so many moral precepts, that we take them for granted and do not realize how many actions of our daily lives are made possible only by moral principles. Why is it safe for you to go into a crowded department store, make a purchase and come out again? The crowd around you needs goods, too; the crowd could easily overpower the few salesgirls, ransack the store and grab your packages and pocketbook as well. Why don't they do it? There is nothing to stop them and nothing to protect you—*except the moral principle of your individual right of life and property.*

Do not make the mistake of thinking that crowds are restrained merely by fear of policemen. There could not be enough policemen in the world if men believed that it is proper and practical to loot. And if men believed this, why shouldn't the policemen believe it, too? Who, then, would be the policemen?

Besides, in a Collectivist society the policemen's duty is not to protect your rights, but to violate them.

It would certainly be expedient for the crowd to loot the department store—if we accept the expediency of the moment as a sound and proper rule of action. But how many department stores, how many factories, farms or homes would we have, and for how long, under this rule of expediency?

If we discard morality and substitute for it the Collectivist doctrine of unlimited majority rule, if we accept the idea that a majority may do anything it pleases, and that anything done by a majority is right *because* it's done by a majority (this being the only standard of right and wrong)—how are men to apply this in practice to their actual lives? Who is the majority? In relation to each particular man, all other men are potential members of that majority which may destroy him at its pleasure at any moment. Then each man and all men become enemies; each has to fear and suspect all; each must try to rob and murder first, before he is robbed and murdered.

If you think that this is just abstract theory, take a look at Europe for a practical demonstration. In Soviet Russia and Nazi Germany, private citizens did the foulest work of the G.P.U. and the Gestapo, spying on one another, delivering their own relatives and friends to the secret police and the torture chambers. *This* was the result in practice of Collectivism in theory. *This* was the concrete application of that empty, vicious Collectivist slogan which seems so high-sounding to the unthinking: "The public good comes above any individual rights."

Without individual rights, no public good is possible.

Collectivism, which places the group above the individual and tells men to sacrifice their rights for the sake of their brothers, results in a state where men have no choice but to dread, hate and destroy their brothers.

Peace, security, prosperity, cooperation and good will among men, all those things considered socially desirable, are possible only under a system of Individualism, where each man is safe in the exercise of his individual rights and in the knowledge that society is there to *protect* his rights, *not* to destroy them. Then each man knows what he may or may not do to his neighbors, and what his neighbors (one or a million of them) may or may not do to him. Then he is free to deal with them as a friend and an equal.

Without a moral code no proper human society is possible.

Without the recognition of individual rights no moral code is possible.
.

11. Is "The Greatest Good For The Greatest Number" A Moral Principle?

"The greatest good for the greatest number" is one of the most vicious slogans ever foisted on humanity.

This slogan has no concrete, specific meaning. There is no way to interpret it benevolently, but a great many ways in which it can be used to justify the most vicious actions.

What is the definition of "the good" in this slogan? None, except: whatever is good for the greatest number. Who, in any particular issue, decides what is good for the greatest number? Why, the greatest number.

If you consider this moral, you would have to approve of the following examples, which are exact applications of this slogan in practice: fifty-one percent of humanity enslaving the other forty-nine; nine hungry cannibals eating the tenth one; a lynching mob murdering a man whom they consider dangerous to the community.

There were seventy million Germans in Germany and six hundred thousand Jews. The greatest number (the Germans) supported the Nazi government which told them that their greatest good would be served by exterminating the smaller number (the Jews) and grabbing their property. This was the horror achieved in practice by a vicious slogan accepted in theory.

But, you might say, the majority in all these examples did not achieve any real good for itself either? No. It didn't. Because "the good" is not determined by counting numbers and is not achieved by the sacrifice of anyone to anyone.

The unthinking believe that this slogan implies something vaguely noble and virtuous, that it tells men to sacrifice themselves for the greatest number of others. If so, should the greatest number of men wish to be virtuous and sacrifice themselves to the smallest number who would be vicious and accept it? No? Well, then should the smallest number be virtuous and sacrifice themselves to the greatest number who would be vicious?

The unthinking assume that every man who mouths this slogan places himself unselfishly with the smaller number to be sacrificed to the greatest number of others. Why should he? There is nothing in the slogan to make him do this. He is much more likely to try to get in with the greatest number, and start sacrificing others. What the slogan actually tells him is that he has no choice, except to rob or be robbed, to crush or get crushed.

The depravity of this slogan lies in the implication that "the good" of a majority must be achieved through the suffering of a minority; that the benefit of one man depends upon the sacrifice of another.

If we accept the Collectivist doctrine that man exists only for the sake of others, then it is true that every pleasure he enjoys (or every bite of food) is evil and immoral if two other men want it. But on this basis men cannot eat, breathe or love (all of that is selfish, and what if two other men want your wife?), men cannot live together at all, and can do nothing except end up by exterminating one another.

Only on the basis of individual rights can any good—private or public—be defined and achieved. Only when each man is free to exist for his own sake—neither sacrificing others to himself nor being sacrificed to others—only then is every man free to work for the greatest good he can achieve for himself by his own choice and by his own effort. And the sum total of such individual efforts is the only kind of general, social good possible.

Do not think that the opposite of "the greatest good for the greatest number" is "the greatest good for the smallest number." The opposite is: the greatest good he can achieve by his own free effort, to every man living.

If you are an Individualist and wish to preserve the American way of life, the greatest contribution you can make is to discard, once and for all, from your thinking, from your speeches, and from your sympathy, the empty slogan of "the greatest good for the greatest number." Reject any argument, oppose any proposal that has nothing but this slogan to justify it. It is a booby-trap. It is a precept of pure Collectivism. You cannot accept it and call yourself an Individualist. Make your choice. It is one or the other.

12. Does The Motive Change The Nature Of A Dictatorship?

The mark of an honest man, as distinguished from a Collectivist, is that he means what he says and knows what he means.

When we say that we hold individual rights to be *inalienable*, we must mean *just that*. *Inalienable* means that which we may not take away, suspend, infringe, restrict or violate—not ever, not at any time, not for any purpose whatsoever.

You cannot say that "man has inalienable rights except in cold weather and on every second Tuesday," just as you cannot say that "man has inalienable rights except in an emergency," or "man's rights cannot be violated except for a good purpose."

Either man's rights are inalienable, or they are not. You cannot say a thing such as "semi-inalienable" and consider yourself either honest or sane. When you begin making conditions, reservations and exceptions, you admit that there is something or someone above man's rights, who may violate them at his discretion. Who? Why, society—that is, the Collective. For what reason? For the good of the Collective. Who decides when rights should be violated? The Collective. If this is what you believe, move over to the side where you belong and admit that you are a Collectivist. Then take all the consequences which Collectivism implies. There is no middle ground here. You cannot have your cake and eat it, too. You are not fooling anyone but yourself.

Do not hide behind meaningless catch-phrases, such as "the middle of the road." Individualism and Collectivism are not two sides of the same road, with a safe rut for you in the middle. They are two roads going into opposite directions. One leads to freedom, justice and prosperity; the other—to slavery, horror and destruction. The choice is yours to make.

The growing spread of Collectivism throughout the world is not due to any cleverness of the Collectivists, but to the fact that most people who oppose them, actually believe in Collectivism themselves. Once a principle is accepted, it is not the man who is half-hearted about it, but the man who is whole-hearted that's going to win; not the man who is least consistent in applying it, but the man who is most consistent. If you enter a race, saying: "I only intend to run the first ten yards," the man who says: "I'll run to the finish line," is going to beat you. When you say: "I only want to violate human rights just a tiny little bit," the communist or fascist who says: "I'm going to destroy all human rights," will beat you and win. You've opened the way for him.

By permitting themselves this initial dishonesty and evasion, men have now fallen into a Collectivist trap, on the question of whether a dictatorship is proper or not. Most people give lip-service to denunciations of dictatorship. But very few take a clear-cut stand and recognize dictatorship for what it is, an absolute evil, in any form, by anyone, for anyone, anywhere, at any time and for any purpose whatsoever.

A great many people now enter into an obscene kind of bargaining about differences between "a good dictatorship" and a "bad dictatorship," about motives, causes or reasons that make dictatorship proper. For the question: "Do you want dictatorship?," the Collectivists have substituted the question: "What kind of dictatorship do you want?" They can afford to let you argue from then on; they have won their point.

A great many people believe that a dictatorship is terrible if it's "for a bad motive," but quite all right and even desirable if it's "for a good motive." Those leaning toward Communism (they usually consider themselves "humanitarians") claim that concentration camps and torture chambers are evil when used "selfishly," "for the sake of one race," as Hitler did, but quite noble when used "unselfishly," "for the sake of the masses," as Stalin does. Those leaning toward Fascism (they usually consider themselves hard-boiled "realists") claim that whips and slave-drivers are impractical when used "inefficiently," as in Russia, but quite practical when used "efficiently," as in Germany.

(And just as an example of where the wrong principle will lead you in practice, observe that the "humanitarians," who are so concerned with relieving the suffering of the masses, endorse, in Russia, a state of misery for a whole population such as no masses have ever had to endure anywhere in history. And the hard-boiled "realists," who are so boastfully eager to be practical, endorse, in Germany, the spectacle of a devastated country in total ruin, the end result of an "efficient" dictatorship.)

When you argue about what is a "good" or a "bad" dictatorship, you have accepted and endorsed the principle of dictatorship. You have accepted a premise of total evil—of *your* right to enslave others for the sake of what *you* think is good. From then on, it's only a question of who will run the Gestapo. You will never be able to reach an agreement with your fellow Collectivists on what is a "good" cause for brutality and what is a "bad" one. Your particular pet definition may not be theirs. You might claim that it is good to slaughter men only for the sake of the poor; somebody else might claim that it is good to slaughter men only for the sake of the rich; you might claim that it is immoral to slaughter anyone except members of a certain class; somebody else might claim that it is immoral to slaughter anyone except members of a certain race. All you will agree on is the slaughter. And that is all you will achieve.

Once you advocate the principle of dictatorship, you invite all men to do the same. If they do not want your particular kind or do not like your particular "good motive," they have no choice but to rush to beat you to it and establish their own kind for their own "good motive," to enslave you before you enslave them. A "good dictatorship" is a contradiction in terms.

The issue is not: for what purpose is it proper to enslave men? The issue is: is it proper to enslave men or not?

There is an unspeakable moral corruption in saying that a dictatorship can be justified by "a good motive" or "an unselfish motive." All the brutal and criminal tendencies which mankind—through centuries of slow climbing out of savagery—has learned to recognize as evil and impractical, have now taken refuge under a "social" cover. Many men now believe that it is evil to rob, murder and torture for one's own sake, but virtuous to do so for the sake of others. You may not indulge in brutality for your own gain, they say, but go right ahead if it's for the gain of others. Perhaps the most revolting statement one can ever hear is: "Sure, Stalin has butchered millions, but it's justifiable, since it's for the benefit of the masses." Collectivism is the last stand of savagery in men's minds.

Do not ever consider Collectivists as "sincere but deluded idealists." The proposal to enslave some men for the sake of others is not an ideal; brutality is not "idealistic," no matter what its purpose. Do not ever say that the desire to "do good" by force is a good motive. Neither power-lust nor stupidity are good motives.

The Fascist New Frontier

*Ayn Rand delivered this lecture at the Ford Hall Forum in Boston in
1962.*

Ladies and gentlemen. I will begin by making a small experiment:
I will read to you some proposals taken from a political program and
ask you to consider, as you hear each proposal, whether you agree
with it or not:

"We ask that the government undertake the obligation above all of
providing citizens with adequate opportunity for employment and earning a living."

"The activities of the individual must not be allowed to clash with
the interests of the community, but must take place within its confines
and be for the good of all. Therefore, we demand: . . . *an end to the
power of the financial interests.*"

"We demand profit sharing in big business."

"We demand a broad extension of care for the aged."

"We demand . . . the greatest possible consideration of small business in the purchases of the national, state, and municipal governments."

"In order to make possible to every capable and industrious [citi-
zen] the attainment of higher education and thus the achievement of a
post of leadership, the government must provide an all-around enlarge-
ment of our entire system of public education. . . . We demand the education at government expense of gifted children of poor parents . . ."

"The government must undertake the improvement of public
health—by protecting mother and child, by prohibiting child labor . . .
by the greatest possible support for all clubs concerned with the physical education of youth."

"[We] combat the . . . materialistic spirit within and without us, and
are convinced that a permanent recovery of our people can only proceed from within on the foundation of

"The Common Good Before the Individual Good." [1]

Do you agree with this program and with its over-all intention and
spirit? Would you be prepared to say that it is a fine, progressive, liberal program? Observe that all of its proposals are being advocated

[1] *Der Nationalsozialismus Dokumente 1933-1945,* edited by Walther Hofer, Fischer Bucherei,
Frankfurt am Main, 1957. (pp. 29-31)

and most of them have been enacted into law in this country.

Ladies and gentlemen, these proposals are from the program of the National Socialist (Nazi) Party of Germany, adopted in Munich, on February 24, 1920.

A science which has all but vanished from our universities—political philosophy—would have spared you any astonishment and would have prevented our country from sliding as far as it has down that kind of road. Political philosophy would have taught people to recognize fundamental premises under any superficial variations. It would have told them that the same moral-political principles will have the same practical results in any age, culture or country that adopts them.

Let me give you some examples of the moral-political principles that dominate today's culture.

I wonder how many of you would disagree with the following declaration: "It is thus necessary that the individual should finally come to realize that his own ego is of no importance in comparison with the existence of his nation; that the position of the individual ego is conditioned solely by the interests of the nation as a whole; that pride and conceitedness, the feeling that the individual . . . is superior, so far from being merely laughable, involve great dangers for the existence of the community that is a nation; that above all the unity of a nation's spirit and will are worth far more than the freedom of the spirit and will of an individual; and that the higher interests involved in the life of the whole must here set the limits and lay down the duties of the interests of the individual."

Most of today's intellectuals, both "conservatives" and "liberals," would subscribe to this expression of the altruist-collectivist creed. It was said by Adolf Hitler, on October 1, 1933.[2]

Now would you remember who said the following: "That is the choice that our nation must make—a choice that lies . . . between the public interest and private comfort—between national greatness and national decline—between the fresh air of progress and the stale, dank atmosphere of 'normalcy'—between dedication or mediocrity." It was said by Senator John F. Kennedy, in his acceptance speech, acknowledging his nomination as Presidential candidate, on July 15, 1960.

Does that awaken any echoes in your memory? Do you remember who regarded "normalcy" as "mediocrity," scorned "private comfort"

[2] *Adolf Hitler from Speeches 1933-1938,* Terramare Office, Berlin, 1938, (pp. 61f)

in the name of "national greatness," and demanded the production of guns instead of butter? It was Goering.

To whom would you ascribe the authorship of the following: "If we then understand national solidarity aright, we cannot but see that it is based on the idea of sacrifice. In other words, if somebody or other objects that the continual giving involves too heavy a burden, then we must reply that . . . true national solidarity cannot find its sense in mere taking." Adolf Hitler said this, on September 30, 1934.[3]

On January 20, 1961, in his inaugural address, President Kennedy said: "And so, my fellow Americans: ask not what America will do for you—ask what you can do for your country."

Here is another item."Once the whole nation has really succeeded in grasping the fact that these measures call for a sacrifice on the part of each individual, then they will lead to something far greater than a mere lessening of material needs, from them will grow the conviction that the 'community of the nation' is no mere empty concept, but that it is something which really is vital and living," said Adolf Hitler.[4]

"But the New Frontier of which I speak," said Senator John F. Kennedy, "is not a set of promises—it is a set of challenges. It sums up not what I intend to offer to the American people, but what I intend to ask of them. . . . It holds out the promise of more sacrifice instead of more security."

Fascism, said Mussolini, is "a life in which the individual, through the denial of himself, through the sacrifice of his own private interests . . . realizes that completely spiritual existence in which his value as a man lies."

The highest principle of Nazism, said Goering, is: "Common good comes before private good."

Now who said: "Private rights are important but the public interest is a greater right"? It was Mr. Paul Rand Dixon, chairman of our Federal Trade Commission. *(The N.Y. Times,* February 11, 1962.)

On September 18, 1962, Generalissimo Francisco Franco of Spain declared that "his regime would seek a 'just distribution' of the national income and equality of opportunities and sacrifices for all." *(The N.Y. Times,* September 19, 1962.)

President Kennedy finds it a little harder. According to *The N.Y. Times* (September 27, 1962), he said that "he was confident of victory

[3] *Ibid.* (p. 70)
[4] *Ibid.*

in the cold war and that any necessary sacrifices would be made. However, he said, he did not know how to distribute these sacrifices equitably in a free society."

(Observe that any social movement which begins by "redistributing" income, ends up by distributing sacrifices.)

The basic moral-political principle running through all these statements is clear: the subordination and sacrifice of the individual to the collective.

That principle (derived from the ethics of altruism) is the ideological root of all statist systems, in any variation, from welfare statism to a totalitarian dictatorship. In today's intellectual chaos—when all political viewpoints agree on a single absolute: to permit no clear definitions of any political concepts—most people believe that the "liberals" lean toward some diluted version of socialism. Although the "liberal" leadership seems to know better, most of the rank-and-file "liberals" believe it, too—or anxiously hope so. The grim historical joke is on them: the New Frontier, which they dare not fully identify, is not a version of socialism, but of fascism.

The difference between these two is superficial and purely formal, but it is significant psychologically: it brings the authoritarian nature of a planned economy crudely into the open.

The main characteristic of socialism (and of communism) is public ownership of the means of production, and, therefore, the abolition of private property. The right to property is the right of use and disposal. Under fascism, men retain the semblance or pretense of private property, but the government holds total power over its use and disposal.

The dictionary definition of *fascism* is: "a governmental system with strong centralized power, permitting no opposition or criticism, controlling all affairs of the nation (industrial, commercial, etc.), emphasizing an aggressive nationalism . . . ."

Under fascism, citizens retain the responsibilities of owning property, without freedom to act and without any of the advantages of ownership. Under socialism, government officials acquire all the advantages of ownership, without any of the responsibilities, since they do not hold title to the property, but merely the right to use it—at least until the next purge. In either case, the government officials hold the economic, political and legal power of life or death over the citizens.

Needless to say, under either system, the inequalities of income and standard of living are greater than anything possible under a free economy—and a man's position is determined, not by his productive ability and achievement, but by political pull and force.

Under both systems, sacrifice is invoked as a magic, omnipotent solution in any crisis—and "the public good" is the altar on which victims are immolated. But there are stylistic differences of emphasis. The socialist-communist axis keeps promising to achieve abundance, material comfort and security for its victims, in some indeterminate future. The fascist-Nazi axis scorns material comfort and security, and keeps extolling some undefined sort of spiritual duty, service and conquest. The socialist-communist axis offers its victims an alleged social ideal. The fascist-Nazi axis offers nothing but loose talk about some unspecified form of *racial* or *national* "greatness." The socialist-communist axis proclaims some grandiose economic plan, which keeps receding year by year. The fascist-Nazi axis merely extols leadership—leadership without purpose, program or direction—and power for power's sake.

Which of these two styles and policies fits Mr. Kennedy's administration?

After two years, have you any clearer idea of what is meant by "The New Frontier" than you had when you first heard it? The only thing which has become clear is Mr. Kennedy's demands for power and ever more discretionary power.

I said that the "liberal" leadership, that is, Mr. Kennedy and his advisers, seem to know the direction in which they are going—if one judges by their efforts not to let anyone else discover it. The style of their public communications—their *"dialogues,"* as they call it—is a carefully calculated mesh of equivocations, approximations and generalities which are slightly off-focus, which are not clear enough for them to be accused of saying what they do say, but just enough to register a certain suggestion, as if they intended to condition the listener, not by means of words, but by means of the unsaid between the lines.

Although Mr. Kennedy's theoretical or philosophical speeches have provoked criticism and resentment, insufficient attention has been paid to their meaning—and yet they are enormously significant.

Mr. Kennedy is waging an ideological war against ideology. The brashly cynical tone of his attempts seems to convey the impatience of an "activist" who is seeking to brush aside the most dangerous barrier to any ruler's ambition: men's *intellect* and its weapons—*political principles.*

Consider, for instance, Mr. Kennedy's address at Yale University, on June 11, 1962.

In the 1930s, the advocates of capitalism were warning this country that the politico-economic principles of the welfare state would necessarily lead to growing government controls and, ultimately, to a totalitarian dictatorship. The "liberals" denied it vehemently. Today, when these predictions are coming true, Mr. Kennedy's sole answer is that the principles are not applicable any longer because these are the 1960s, not the 1930s.

In that speech, Mr. Kennedy was begging his audience to drop such "illusions" as conceptual knowledge, theories, principles, abstractions, and to consider only the specific problems of our day, singly, never relating one problem to another. This means: to adopt the concrete-bound mentality of a Babbitt or a savage who does not look past the range of the immediate moment, sees nothing but immediate problems, and solves them without reference to any principles, usually by means of a club.

No caricature of a Babbitt could project quite so venomous a hatred of the intellect. "Illusions," "truisms," "stereotypes," "myths," "cliches," "platitudes," "slogans," "labels," "incantations," "rhetoric" are the terms Mr. Kennedy used to describe—what? Since he avoided naming it explicitly, one has to read his entire speech to discover the enemy on whom all that abuse was poured. The enemy is philosophy, ideology, principles, ideas—or any man who applies them to political problems.

It was not against any particular ideology that that speech was directed, but against ideology as such. It was not businessmen or Republicans that Mr. Kennedy was denouncing, but all those who raise the obstacle of principles in the path of governmental action.

The example of Western Europe, he asserted, shows that "governments, prepared to face technical problems without ideological preconceptions, can coordinate the elements of a national economy to bring about unexampled growth and prosperity."

What causes economic growth? What is the source of prosperity? How does one "coordinate" a national economy? All such questions are irrelevant, according to Mr. Kennedy; a government should act, rule, control, unhampered by any theoretical knowledge; political science and economics are "ideological preconceptions."

As an example of a specific, practical, non-ideological problem, Mr. Kennedy offered the following: "How in sum, can we make our free economy work at full capacity—that is, provide adequate profits for enterprise, adequate wages for labor, adequate utilization of plant and adequate opportunity for all?"

Since all politico-economic principles are to be discarded, by what standard does one determine what is "adequate"? And who determines it? Mr. Kennedy did not say.

"Economics is secondary," said Adolf Hitler on September 18, 1922. "The history of the world teaches us that no people has become great through economics, but, indeed, has perished on its account." [5]

Mr. Kennedy seems to agree; economic theories, he suggests, are irrelevant to the task of ruling a nation.

"What is at stake in our economic decisions today," said Mr. Kennedy, "is not some grand warfare of rival ideologies, but the practical management of the modern economy."

At a time when every country in the world (including the enslaved ones) is torn by the life-and-death struggle of two opposite ideologies—freedom versus statism—Mr. Kennedy permits himself to sneer at "some grand warfare of rival ideologies." Since he could not possibly mean that that global conflict has, somehow, by-passed our country, there is only one other thing that he could have meant: that, for us, the conflict is over, and statism—a government-managed economy—has won.

"The differences today are mainly matters of degree," he stated. "And we cannot understand and attack our contemporary problems if we are bound by the traditional labels and worn-out slogans of an earlier era."

If we don't use any "labels"—which means: if we never identify the nature of different political systems—we will not discover that we

[5] *Sozialismus wie ihn der Fuhrer sieht,* edited by F. Meystre, Heerschild-verlag, Munich, 1935.

are accepting statism, or notice how that switch is pulled on us.

"Each sector of activity must be approached on its own merits," said Mr. Kennedy, "and in terms of specific national needs. Generalities in regard to Federal expenditures therefore can be misleading— each case, science, urban renewal, education, agriculture, natural resources—each case must be determined on its own merits if we are to profit from our unrivaled ability to combine the strength of public and private agencies, public and private purposes—public and private interests."

When has *that* been "our unrivaled ability"? Such a "combination" is precisely what the American system—a free economy—was *not* designed to be and cannot support for long. A "mixed economy," a mixture of freedom and controls, is an unstable "combination" anywhere, but particularly unsuccessful here, in America—as witness our falling rate of economic growth. The United States was the freest economy in the history of the world. Though some government controls did remain, they were marginal, at first, and contradictory to the rest of the system. It was the growth of those controls and contradictions that gradually wrecked our economy—yet, in an oddly casual aside, Mr. Kennedy is slipping in the suggestion that government controls were the distinctive characteristic of the American way of life.

That suggestion was strengthened in his speech a few paragraphs later.

"The solid ground of mutual confidence," said Mr. Kennedy, "is the necessary partnership of government with all the sectors of our society in the steady quest for economic progress."

"Partnership" is an indecent euphemism for "government control." There can be no partnership between armed bureaucrats and defenseless private citizens who have no choice but to obey. What chance would you have against a "partner" whose word—whose *arbitrary* word—is law, who may give you a hearing (if your pressure group is big enough), but who will play favorites and bargain your interests away, who will always have the last word and the legal "right" to enforce it on you at the point of a gun, holding your property, your work, your future, your life in his power? Is *that* the meaning of "partnership"? Does such a use of language contribute to the clarity of our national "dialogue"?

Government control over "all sectors of a society" is the essence of the totalitarian state in any of its forms: fascism, communism, Nazism, socialism and any "mixed" economy on its sliding way to one of those major four. "The differences are mainly matters of degree."

No, Mr. Kennedy does not believe that the ideological switch has already been accomplished. That is what his speech was striving to accomplish. It is on the last, transitional lap of that fatal slide that it becomes important to silence ideological discussions.

Such is Mr. Kennedy's view—and preview—of our economy.

It is not an unprecedented view. Hermann Messerschmidt gave the following description of the Nazi view of *their* economy:

"I. The economy serves the state and thus the people. It is a national economy, thus, an economic order whose tasks and goals are determined by national events.

"1. On the one hand, it is not a state economy, i.e., not an economy administered as a whole by the state.

"2. On the other hand, it is not an economy of social interests, which in complete self-sufficiency from the state seeks only the highest good of the individual.

"3. On the contrary, it is controlled and free at the same time.

a) The economy is controlled because it is unconditionally obliged to serve the laws of national life.

b) The economy is free because within it personal creativity and accomplishment can fully develop."[6]

Clear, isn't it?

This sort of verbal chaos—this unintelligible scramble of political terms, which denies that controls are controls and pays lip-service to freedom—is typical of fascism. It is also typical of the New Frontier.

Mr. Kennedy's address at Yale seemed to be part of an attempt to pull an intellectual coup d'état.

Mr. Kennedy and his advisers seem determined to cash in on our cultural bankruptcy and on the cowardice of their opponents. An intellectual coup d'état would consist of the following: keep switching the meaning of political concepts until they dissolve in an unintelligible fog—get people conditioned subliminally to accept the implications of the doctrines you would not dare proclaim explicitly—then

[6] Reprinted in *Der Nationalsozialismus Dokumente 1933-1945, op cit.* (p. 84)

let them wake up some morning to a fait accompli, to the astonished realization: "Why, everybody knows that freedom is slavery and that Americanism is statism."

There are other examples of the odd little touches that seem to suggest Mr. Kennedy's attempt to rewrite the ideological history of the United States.

On April 11, 1962, in his televised denunciation of the steel industry for raising its prices, Mr. Kennedy made the following remark: "Price and wage decisions in this country . . . are and ought to be freely and privately made. But the American people have a right to expect, *in return for that freedom,* a higher sense of business responsibility for the welfare of their country. . ." (Italics mine)

Here is an explicit declaration by the President of the United States that *freedom* is not an inalienable right of the individual, but a conditional favor or privilege granted to him by society (by "the people" or the collective)—a privilege which he has to purchase by performing some sort of duty *in return.* Should he fail in that duty, "the people" have the "right" to abrogate his freedom and return him to his natural condition of slavery. Rights, according to this concept, are the property of the collective, not of the individual. *This* is the basic principle of statism. A remark of that kind could not have been mere rhetorical carelessness on the part of Mr. Kennedy who prides himself on his knowledge of history.

Where were the "conservatives" on April 11, when Mr. Kennedy slapped the Declaration of Independence in its philosophical face? Probably the same place they were on the Fourth of July, which he chose as the day to commit the mean little indignity of making a speech entitled "The Declaration of Interdependence."

Now observe the semantics of the "dialogues" that preceded the steel crisis. Secretary Goldberg announced, as a "definitive" statement of the Kennedy administration's philosophy, that the government henceforth would "define and assert the national interest" in issues of collective bargaining. He declared that labor-management relations should no longer be resolved "on the old testing ground of clash of selfish interest," and he made it clear that the *new* testing ground would involve *three* clashing interests: the selfish interest of management, the selfish interest of labor and the (unselfish?) interest of "the nation," as enunciated by the government.

Observe the hypocritical euphemism of such a phrase as the intention *"to define and assert the national interest."* Anybody can define and assert anything he pleases—so this is obviously not what the phrase was intended to mean. If it were, Mr. Kennedy would not have flown into a rage when the steel industry ignored the government's assertion. The phrase meant—and was so intended to be understood, but not publicly translated—that "the national interest" is whatever the government chooses to say it is and that any assertion of the government's wishes is a command.

No, Congress had never passed any law giving Mr. Kennedy the power to dictate prices and wages. But it had passed many non-objective laws, such as antitrust, which gave him the power to crack down on any dissenter and to make legality obsolete.

The German Reichstag voted itself out of existence. Our Congress seems to have achieved the same end piecemeal—gradually and cumulatively.

The authoritarian violence of Mr. Kennedy's behavior was too much for most people: its overtones were too obvious. *Time* magazine called it "one of the most savage sustained attacks ever launched by a U.S. President against big business"—and mentioned "the almost totalitarian thrust of his attack." (April 20, 1962.)

The New Republic, which is not exactly pro-business, published an excellent article by Charles A. Reich, entitled "Another Such Victory . . ." (April 30, 1962.) "In a free society," wrote Professor Reich, "there can be no unitary public interest, no single, authoritatively fixed idea of 'the public good.' Freedom has little meaning if it only allows action that 'responsibly' conforms to the President's idea of the national interest." And further: "Will business now come crawling to the government to seek its pleasure? And, what is more important, will individual citizens fear to disagree with 'national policy'? President Kennedy's victory may have advanced peace and plenty, but it did no service to freedom."

Is freedom a part of Mr. Kennedy's program?

The dividing line—the *frontier*—between a "mixed economy" and a dictatorship lies in the issue of freedom of speech; the establishment of censorship is the tombstone of a free country. Observe the concerted efforts of the administration to push—or rather, to smuggle—us across *that* particular frontier.

I say "to smuggle," because these efforts are as devious as the New Frontiersmen's use of language—and the fog of their terminology is here at its thickest.

The advance member of the border patrol, struggling diligently to stretch the barbed-wire lines, is Newton N. Minow, Chairman of the Federal Communications Commission. His task, apparently, is to pull a crucial switch in the realm of free speech: first, to obliterate the distinction between private action and governmental action, and then to invert their meaning. It is an old collectivist switch, but it has not been asserted quite so openly before.

Freedom of speech means freedom from interference, suppression or punitive action by the government—and nothing else. It does not mean the right to demand the financial support or the material means to express your views at the expense of other men who may not wish to support you. Freedom of speech includes the freedom not to agree, not to listen and not to support one's own antagonists. A "right" does not include the material implementation of that right by other men; it includes only the freedom to earn that implementation by one's own effort. Private citizens cannot use physical force or coercion; they cannot *censor* or *suppress* anyone's views or publications. Only the government can do so. And *censorship* is a concept that pertains *only* to governmental action.

Mr. Minow is trying to reverse that concept.

Mr. Minow has announced officially that any television or radio station which does not satisfy his unstated criterion of an unspecified *"public* service," will lose its license, that is: will be silenced forever.

This, Mr. Minow claims, is *not* censorship. What *is* censorship, then? Believe it or not, censorship is a sponsor's refusal to finance a television program, or a station's refusal to broadcast a program, or a publisher's refusal to publish a book—and it is the government's duty to *"protect"* us from such infringements of our "freedom."

Such is the "protection-racket" from the other side of the New Frontier: the views, the ideas, the convictions, the choices of private individuals on the use and disposal of their own material means—of their own property—are censorship. What, then, is non-censorship? Mr.

Minow's edicts.

This is a clear illustration of why human rights cannot exist without property rights, and how the destruction of property rights leads to the destruction of all rights and all freedom. If the New Frontiersmen succeed in obliterating in people's minds the difference between economic power and political power, between a private choice and a government order, between intellectual persuasion and physical force—they can then establish the ultimate collectivist inversion: the claim that a *private* action is coercion, but a governmental action is freedom.

I should like to quote from an article I wrote on this subject in the March 1962 issue of *The Objectivist Newsletter:*

"It is true, as Mr. Minow assures us, that he does not propose to establish censorship; what he proposes is much worse. Censorship, in its old-fashioned meaning, is a government edict that forbids the discussion of some specific subjects or ideas—an edict enforced by the government's scrutiny of all forms of communication prior to their public release. But for stifling the freedom of men's minds the modern method is much more potent: it rests on the power of non-objective law; it neither forbids nor permits anything; it never defines or specifies; it merely delivers men's lives, fortunes, careers, ambitions into the arbitrary power of a bureaucrat who can reward or punish at whim."

In a recent issue of *Barron's* magazine (December 10, 1962), you will find factual evidence to support and illustrate my statement. "Last week," writes *Barron's,* "the bureaucrat who uses words so well [Mr. Minow] for once was speechless. For the staff of FCC, taking their cue from their outspoken leader, had been caught sending letters of alarming frankness to television stations throughout the country. Unless they proved properly receptive to the agency's views on the content and timing of programs, the message suggested, they might have trouble getting their licenses renewed. . . . The magazine *Broadcasting,* which exposed the whole affair, bluntly called it 'another step toward centralized program control' and 'blatant coercion.' "

Mr. Minow is not the only prominent member of the New Frontier's border patrol; there is another, older one who has been waiting for many years for a frontier of just that kind.

On July 15, 1962, *The N.Y. Times* carried a story announcing that: "An Antitrust panel of the House Judiciary Committee is preparing a broad inquiry on the press and other news media." The head of that inquiry is Representative Emanuel Celler.

"We are very much aware of the First Amendment," Mr. Celler declared. "We are also aware that the courts have said you can distinguish between the business practices and the editorial operations of newspapers."

Apparently, Mr. Celler regarded a declaration of his "awareness" as sufficient compliance with the Constitution—because he then proceeded to announce that the inquiry will deal with such (non-editorial?) issues as the "handling of news and the impact of syndicated columns on the gathering and presentation of local news."

Mr. Celler will also investigate the fact that in some cities one man or company owns both the morning and evening newspapers.

"We shall endeavor to find out," he stated, "whether, in those cities, the news is slanted according to the prejudice or idiosyncrasies of those common owners; whether the editorial policy is consistently politically slanted." (A noneditorial issue?)

Does this mean that the owner of a newspaper has no right to hold *consistent* political convictions and that a newspaper is not entitled to a *consistent* editorial policy? If the owner of one newspaper possesses the right of free speech, does he lose it if he acquires two newspapers? Who determines what is "slanted" and which political views are "prejudice or idiosyncrasies"? The government?

"Also," declared Mr. Celler, "we are interested in seeing whether or to what extent the columnists might be drying up local talent in assaying the news of the day."

Well, it is incontestably certain that the talents of the local "High School Bugle" could not possibly compete with nationally syndicated columnists.

Here we see the essence of the antitrust doctrines—in so grotesque a form that no satirist would venture to offer it as a caricature. Yet it is not a caricature, it is the naked, brutal truth.

If it is right to sacrifice ability to incompetence, or success to failure, or achievement to envy—if it is right to break up giant industrial concerns because smaller companies cannot compete with them—then it is right to silence every man who has acquired a national audience and clear the field for those whose audience will never grow beyond the corner drugstore.

If it is right to deprive the small towns of the wider choice and lower prices offered by the big chain stores, and force them to support the "little corner grocer"—then it is right to deprive them of any intellectual contact with the nation, of any famous voices, of any TV network programs, and confine them by law to the news of local Rummage Sales and Ice Cream Socials, to the "assaying" of such news by cracker-barrel pundits, and to the poetry recitals of the League of Mrs. Worthington's Daughters.

Freedom of speech? "Why, we don't deprive any man of his freedom of speech," the trustbusters would chorus, "provided he is not heard beyond the boundaries of his township or of his city block."

No, the government would not establish any censorship; it would not need to. The threat of antitrust prosecutions will be sufficient. We have seen what it did to the steel industry. Rule by hidden, unprovable intimidation relies on the victims' "voluntary" self-enslavement. The result is worse than a censored press: it is a servile press.

These are examples of the theoretical spadework along the New Frontier. For an early preview of the practical results, consider the news blackout during the recent Cuban crisis, and the official attempt to manipulate news "as an instrument of public policy."

Ladies and gentlemen, no dictatorship—neither Nazi Germany nor Soviet Russia nor any other—has ever abolished freedom of speech at a single sudden stroke: it has always been done by a series of gradual steps, like the ones just described.

What makes any of it possible? That magic passkey which opens—and locks—the gates of a totalitarian state: *"the public interest";* the concept of a "public interest" that demands the sacrifice of individual rights and lives.

Mr. Kennedy and his advisers are not the only ones who uphold that collectivist doctrine. It is shared by virtually all of our political leaders, "liberals" and "conservatives" alike. It was invoked by Republicans in the nineteenth century, as a justification for the growth of government controls of the particular controls which *they* favored. The Sherman Antitrust Act—the most destructive of our statutes—was passed by a Republican congress and, to this day, is supported by most "conservatives."

Mr. Kennedy's administration is not the cause, but the effect and the *product* of a long collectivist trend. It is the ultimate result of a "mixed economy." A "mixed economy" is an institutionalized civil war of pressure groups that fight for special legislative favors at one another's expense and thus create an ever accelerating growth of government controls.

In this respect, Mr. Kennedy is not an innovator, not a New Frontiersman, but a panicky defender of the status quo—the untenable, collapsing status quo of the last stages of a "mixed economy." He is not for or against business, or labor, or any other group. Since he is expected to "reconcile" the contradictory demands of *all* pressure groups, he has no choice but to seek arbitrary power and to act on the blind expediency of any given moment. There is no way to reconcile the irreconcilable or to make the unworkable work; in such conditions, there is nothing to seek but power for power's sake.

The guiltiest ideological school today are the welfare-statists who claim that they are not socialists, that they had never advocated or intended the socialization of private property, that they want to "preserve" private property—with government control of its use and disposal. But *that* is the fundamental characteristic of fascism.

It makes no difference whether government controls allegedly favor the interests of labor or business, of the poor or the rich, of a special class or a special race: the results are the same. The notion that a dictatorship can benefit any one social group at the expense of others is a worn remnant of the Marxist mythology of class warfare, refuted by half-a-century of factual evidence. All men are victims and losers under a dictatorship; nobody wins except the ruling clique.

Mr. Kennedy may be right in one respect: when he declares that "the differences today are mainly matters of degree," he is right in regard to the so-called "practical" politicians and party platforms of the immediate present. It is true that all the advocates of a "mixed economy," "liberal" or "conservative," Democratic or Republican, have accepted the basic principles of statism and that the differences among them *are* only matters of degree—and of time: some wish to gallop, others to crawl toward the same abyss. In this respect, Mr. Kennedy is merely cashing in on their evasions and confronting them *explicitly* with the consequences of what they had been advocating *implicitly.* But, like the rest of them, what Mr. Kennedy does not care to name explicitly is the fact that the system emerging from their haphazard, piecemeal efforts is *fascism.*

Mr. Kennedy's public "posture" and speeches are designed to condition us to the notion that his "nameless" system is our only alternative to communism—that our only choice is a choice of rulers—that the totalitarian state is here to stay—that the possibility of a free, noncoercive society, the society of *capitalism,* has collapsed or vanished or had never existed and is not to be discussed or considered.

Hitler rose to power by claiming that Nazism was the only alternative to communism and that the age of freedom was past.

But, in fact, it is statism that has collapsed as an intellectual power or a cultural ideal. The altruist-collectivist creed has run its course. The twentieth century has seen its climax and the end of its inhuman trail. The New Frontier is only a feeble afterglow—a worn, tired, cynical remnant, patched from scraps along that trail. In today's intellectual vacuum, it holds a position of leadership only by default.

If you wish to oppose it, you must challenge its basic premises. You must begin by realizing that there is no such thing as "the public interest" except as the sum of the interests of individual men. And the basic, common interest of all men—all *rational* men—is freedom. *Freedom* is the first requirement of "the public interest"—not *what* men do when they are free, but *that* they are free. All their achievements rest on that foundation—and cannot exist without it.

The principles of a free, non-coercive social system are the only form of "the public interest." Such principles did and do exist. Try to project such a system. In today's cultural atmosphere, it might appear to you like a journey into the unknown. But—like Columbus—what you will discover is America.

Modern Management

This is Ayn Rand's response to the question "what is or should be the nature of the 'faith' subscribed to by modern management?" printed in The Atlantic Economic Review, *September 1958.*

The modern businessman needs a new philosophy of life and a new code of morality—a morality based on reason and self-interest. The "Protestant Ethic," as described in *The Organization Man*, was not a philosophical code of morality. It was a popular make-shift, a bootleg set of rules for "practical" action—and, from the start, it was fighting a losing war against the official morality of the Judaic-Christian tradition: the morality of altruism, mysticism, and self-immolation to the welfare of others. Capitalism is incompatible with the morality of altruism—and what we are seeing now is the last stage of their conflict.

The world crisis of our age is the result, the climax and the dead-end of the altruist code. Businessmen—and wider: all men of ability—are its first victims. When *need*, rather than achievement, is regarded as a primary moral claim, it is not the "meek" but the *mediocre* who inherit the earth.

The source of the disaster lies in our modern philosophy. The essence of pragmatism, Positivism, Scientism and all the rest of the neo-mystic, Platonic schools of non-thought, is a single basic theory: that man's mind is impotent, that reason is an illusion and that objective reality does not exist, or, if it does, man has no power ever to perceive it. If you regard this as harmless, academic speculation, take a look at the pages of *The Organization Man* and you will see that the miserable little socialized, self-abnegating mediocrities described by Mr. Whyte are the exact, practical realization of those philosophical theories. After years of being battered, in school and college, with the question: "Who are you to know?", the average young man will regard himself as a helpless zombie and will seek obedience to the group as his only road to safety. The next and final step is for communist Russia—or any other consistent exponent of an anti-mind, anti-self philosophy—to take him over.

If the American businessman has had a tendency to be anti-intellectual, it is the above kind of philosophers who have made him so. He knew that one cannot live by such philosophies and he committed the tragic error of attempting to live without any philosophy. This is his greatest mistake: that he regards as intellectuals men whose sole claim to the title is their denial of the intellect.

What we need now is a union of the intellectual and the businessman. We need a *new type of intellectuals*, men who are thinkers, men not of some super-reality, but of this earth—in short, Aristotelians. Platonism, in one version or another, was the philosophy of all the dark ages and of all the collectivist dictatorships in history. Aristotelianism was the father of the Renaissance, of the Industrial Revolution, of science, of individualism, of capitalism and of the United States.

If the real businessmen—the first-raters—will give one hour of their eighteen-hour work-day to consider the nature and the power of philosophy, they will see that the base is being cut from under their feet, that the rest of their time—as well as most of their public speeches—is given to the support, the financing and the glorification of their own destroyers. Then let them challenge the reign of entrenched mediocrity. Let them stop preaching their enemy's creed. Let them stop apologizing for their ability and their success. Let them stop seeking the collectivist sanction of "public service." Let them proclaim their *moral* right to exist and to earn a profit.

In short, let them check their philosophical premises—and their Public Relations Departments.

The Only Path to Tomorrow

An edited version of this article appeared in The Reader's Digest, *January 1944.*

The greatest threat to mankind and civilization is the spread of the totalitarian philosophy. Its best ally is not the devotion of its followers but the confusion of its enemies. To fight it, we must understand it.

Totalitarianism is collectivism. Collectivism means the subjugation of the individual to a group—whether to a race, class or state does not matter. Collectivism holds that man must be chained to collective action and collective thought for the sake of what is called "the common good."

Throughout history no tyrant ever rose to power except on the claim of representing "the common good." Horrors which no man would dare consider for his own selfish sake are perpetrated with a clear conscience by "altruists" who justify themselves by—the common good.

No tyrant has ever lasted long by force of arms alone. Men have been enslaved primarily by spiritual weapons. And the greatest of these is the collectivist doctrine of the supremacy of the common good over the individual. No dictator could rise if men held as a sacred faith the conviction that they have inalienable rights of which they cannot be deprived for any cause whatsoever, by any man whatsoever, neither by evil-doer nor benefactor; that no cause is higher than these rights.

Individualism holds that man is an independent entity with an inalienable right to the pursuit of his own happiness in a society where men deal with one another as equals in voluntary, unregulated exchange.

The American system is founded on individualism. If it is to survive, we must understand the principles of individualism and hold them as our standard in any public question, in every issue we face. We must have a positive credo, a clear, consistent faith.

We must learn to reject as total evil the conception that "the common good" is superior to individual rights. General happiness cannot be created out of general suffering and self-immolation. The only happy society is one of happy individuals. One cannot have a healthy forest made up of rotten trees.

The power of society must always be limited by the basic, inalienable rights of the individual. Such was the conception of the founders of our country, who placed individual rights above any and all collective claims.

The right of liberty means man's right to individual action, individual choice, individual initiative and individual property. Without the right to private property no independent action is possible.

The right to the pursuit of happiness means man's right to live for himself, to choose what constitutes his own, private, personal happiness and to work for its achievement. Each individual is the sole and final judge in this choice. A man's happiness cannot be prescribed to him by another man or by any number of other men.

These rights are the unconditional, personal, private, individual possession of every man, granted to him by the fact of his birth and requiring no other sanction.

From the beginning of history, two antagonists have stood face to face, two opposite types of men: the Active and the Passive. The Active Man is the producer, the creator, the originator, the individualist. His basic need is independence—in order to think and work. He neither needs nor seeks power over other men—nor can he be made to work under any form of compulsion. Every type of good work—from laying bricks to writing a symphony—is done by the Active Man. Degrees of human ability vary, but the basic principle remains the same; the degree of a man's independence and initiative determines his talent as a worker and his worth as a man.

The Passive Man is found on every level of society, in mansions and in slums, and his identification mark is his dread of independence. He is a parasite who expects to be taken care of by others, who wishes to be given directives, to obey, to submit, to be regulated, to be told. He welcomes collectivism, which eliminates any chance that he might have to think or act on his own initiative.

When a society is based on the needs of the Passive Man it destroys the Active; but when the Active is destroyed, the Passive cannot survive. When a society is based on the needs of the Active Man, he carries the Passive ones along on his energy and raises them as he rises, as the whole society rises. This has been the pattern of all human progress.

Some humanitarians demand a collectivist state because of their pity for the incompetent or Passive Man. For his sake they wish to harness the Active. But the Active Man cannot function in harness. And once he is destroyed, the destruction of the Passive Man follows automatically. So if pity is the humanitarians' first consideration, then in the name of pity, if nothing else, they should leave the Active Man free to function, in order to help the Passive. There is no other way to help him. The Active, however, are exterminated in a collectivist society.

The history of mankind is the history of the struggle between the Active Man and the Passive, between the individual and the collective. The countries which have produced the happiest men, the highest standards of living and the greatest cultural advances have been the countries where the power of the collective—of the government, of the state—was limited and the individual was given freedom of independent action. As examples: The rise of Rome, with its conception of law based on a citizen's rights, over the collectivist barbarism of its time. The rise of England, with its system of government based on Magna Carta, over the collectivist barbarism of its time. The rise of the United States to a degree of achievement unequaled in history—by grace of the individual freedom and independence which our Constitution gave each citizen against the collective.

While men are still pondering upon the causes of the rise and fall of civilizations, every page of history cries to us that there is but one source of progress: Individual Man in independent action. Collectivism is the ancient principle of savagery. A savage's whole existence is public, ruled by the laws of his tribe. Civilization is the process of setting man free from men.

We are now facing a choice: to go forward or to go back.

Collectivism is not the "New Order of Tomorrow." It is the order of a very dark yesterday. But there is a New Order of Tomorrow. It belongs to Individual Man—the only creator of any tomorrows humanity has ever been granted.

The First Amendment and "Symbolic Speech"

These are Ayn Rand's comments on the controversial Nazi march through the streets of Skokie, Illinois (from The Objectivist Calendar, *June 1978).*

That's a very complex issue. So long as the courts interpret a march through the streets as a form of freedom of speech, so long as communists or leftists or anyone else is permitted to march, the Nazis have to be permitted to do it, too. In this respect, I agree very reluctantly with the [representatives of the] A.C.L.U. (reluctantly, because I seldom agree with them): they do not like the Nazis, but they find they have to fight for the Nazis' "right" to march. If demonstrations are regarded as a form of speech, then anyone and everyone must be permitted.

But what I challenge (and not only because of that particular case) is the interpretation of demonstrations and of other *actions* as so-called "symbolic speech." When you lose the distinction between action and speech, you lose, eventually, the freedom of both. The Skokie case is a good illustration of that principle. There is no such thing as "symbolic speech." You do not have the right to parade through the public streets or to obstruct public thoroughfares. You have the right of assembly, yes, on your own property, and on the property of your adherents or your friends. But nobody has the "right" to clog the streets. The streets are only for passage. The hippies, in the '60s, should have been forbidden to lie down on city pavements. (They used to lie down across a street and cause dreadful traffic snarls, in order to display their views, to attract attention, to register a protest.) If they were permitted to do it, the Nazis should be permitted as well. Properly, both should have been forbidden. They may speak, yes. They may not take action at whim on public property.

I would like to add that the matter of "the overt expression of genocide" is irrelevant to the issue of free speech. The principle of free speech is not concerned with the *content* of a man's speech and does not protect only the expression of *good* ideas, but of *all* ideas. If it were otherwise, who would determine which ideas are good and which are to be forbidden? The government?

Furthermore, there is no principle by which genocide—a crime

117

against a group of men—can be regarded as *morally* different from (or worse than) a crime against an individual: the difference is only quantitative, not moral. It can be easily demonstrated that communism means and requires the extermination—the genocide, if you wish—of a particular human species: the men of ability. The communists and the Nazis are merely two variants of the same evil notion: collectivism. But both should be free to speak—evil ideas are dangerous only by default of men advocating better ideas.

The Secular Meaning of Christmas

This is Ayn Rand's response to the question of whether it is appropriate for an atheist to celebrate Christmas (from The Objectivist Calendar, *December 1976).*

Yes, of course. A national holiday, in this country, cannot have an exclusively religious meaning. The secular meaning of the Christmas holiday is wider than the tenets of any particular religion: it is good will toward men—a frame of mind which is not the exclusive property (though it is supposed to be part, but is a largely unobserved part) of the Christian religion.

The charming aspect of Christmas is the fact that it expresses good will in a cheerful, happy, benevolent, *non-sacrificial* way. One says: "Merry Christmas"—not "Weep and Repent." And the good will is expressed in a material, *earthly* form—by giving presents to one's friends, or by sending them cards in token of remembrance. (The gift-giving is charming only so long as it is non-sacrificial. O. Henry's famous "The Gift of the Magi" is a sadistic horror story, though he did not intend it as such; that story is a good example of the futility of altruism.)

The best aspect of Christmas is the aspect usually decried by the mystics: the fact that Christmas has been *commercialized*. The gift-buying is good for business and good for the country's economy; but, more importantly in this context, it stimulates an enormous outpouring of ingenuity in the creation of products devoted to a single purpose: to give men pleasure. And the street decorations put up by department stores and other institutions—the Christmas trees, the winking lights, the glittering colors—provide the city with a spectacular display, which only "commercial greed" could afford to give us. One would have to be terribly depressed to resist the wonderful gaiety of that spectacle.

Merry Christmas and Happy New Year to all of you.

Favorite Writers

This is Ayn Rand's reply to readers' questions regarding what she reads for pleasure (from The Objectivist Calendar, *April 1977).*

As you probably know, my favorite fiction writers are Victor Hugo, Dostoevsky and O. Henry. I have long since given up reading modern "serious" literature, which is neither serious nor literary. Today, the only kind of fiction that I read for pleasure (as distinguished from reading for information) is popular fiction, specifically mystery stories. But even here, the best writing was done before the 1950s. There are some exceptions, but so rare that I would not advise you to search for them through the shapeless, pretentious and unreadable trash published in the last twenty-five years.

The ability to tell a story and to construct a plot (a *purposeful* progression of events) is very rare, very difficult to use, and requires the characteristic which I enjoy and admire most in a writer: *ingenuity*. Today, one can find it only in mystery stories (not in spy or adventure novels, only in mysteries).

The incomparably best writer of mysteries is Agatha Christie. She has written dozens of novels, and—with the exception of a few, particularly her last ones—they are brilliantly ingenious, intriguing and suspenseful. My favorites are: *Death on the Nile, And Then There Were None, The A.B.C. Murders* and, above all, *The Mysterious Mr. Quin.* (This last is a collection of short stories, and is the best-written of Agatha Christie's books.)

The best stylist among mystery writers is Dorothy L. Sayers. Her story structures are not always good, but she writes beautifully—much, much better than most so-called serious writers. Her best novel: *Murder Must Advertise.*

For ingenious devices, I would recommend Carter Dickson, but with some reservations: I have not read all of his work, and some of his gimmicks are so far-fetched that they border on cheating (by being impossible).

If you have missed his stories on television, Erle Stanley Gardner, the author of Perry Mason [mysteries], is always reliably entertaining. His writing style is somewhat primitive, but this is better than the pre-

120

tentious overwriting of some modern ladies who try to combine mysteries with belle-lettres and kill them both.

A mystery novelist who was very popular in the 1930s is Leslie Ford. She is inventive, imaginative and writes very well—but her novels vary unpredictably: some are very good and some simply awful, so you have to proceed at your own risk.

When one talks about ingenuity, one cannot omit Fredric Brown, who is brilliant in that respect. But the serious flaw in his novels is so malevolent a sense of life that it all but defeats his stories. A sense of life is not the dominant element in a mystery story, but Mr. Brown's is almost too much. (I am speaking of his mysteries, not his science fiction; I do not care for modern science fiction.) Mr. Brown's wittiest and most startling book is a collection of short stories entitled *Nightmares and Geezenstacks*.

Years ago, I liked the early novels of Mickey Spillane, but he has been disintegrating for years and has now descended to the fully modern. I would like to say "Rest in peace," but no peace can be found in four-letter words and pornography.

Another old favorite of mine—Donald Hamilton—has survived. He is still writing, though not quite as entertainingly as he used to. (His novels are adventure stories more than mysteries.)

There are a number of authors who wrote one good mystery, but never repeated its quality, so I will not recommend them. I hope you will find some books to read for pleasure—among the above.

Questions and Answers on *Anthem*

A high school teacher had assigned Anthem, *Ayn Rand's novelette, to her tenth-grade English classes. She wrote to Miss Rand, reporting that her students enjoyed the book because of the "unique ideas and theories presented"; however, the students raised questions about the book which the teacher was unable to answer, and she asked the author for help. Printed below are some of the questions, and Miss Rand's answers. (From* The Objectivist Calendar, *June 1 979).*

Q: Did you model your characters after particular individuals?

AR: No. All the characters are invented by me.

Q: How did you decide upon the names for the characters in the book?

AR: Since the people had no concept of individuality, they could not have individual names—only numbers. I patterned the numbering after telephone numbers, with the prefixes consisting of statist slogans, some good, but hypocritical for that society (such as "Liberty")—others, ironic on my part (such as "Equality" for the hero, who is obviously a genius and is not the intellectual "equal" of average men).

Q: What race is Equality?

AR: Any race—since he represents the best possible to all races of men.

Q: When Equality went into the forest, wasn't he afraid after he heard about those who never returned?

AR: No, he was not afraid, because he had the adventurous courage of a scientist who always wants to study the unknown. Besides, he did not want ever to return to his hometown, to the slavery of a collectivist state.

Q: How were the people in the Unmentionable Times destroyed?

AR: They were destroyed by the kind of philosophy they accepted. They rejected reason, egoism, individualism and freedom—and they accepted mysticism, altruism, collectivism and dictatorship. The society presented in *Anthem* is the ultimate logical consequence and the perfect embodiment of that vicious philosophy. Observe that the slogans of that philosophy are preached all around us today. If you don't like the kind of society you saw in *Anthem*, it is that philosophy that you have to reject and oppose.

Q: How can the Council of Scholars make decisions without thinking?

AR: They make decisions by the guidance of their feelings and by blind obedience to a government—prescribed dogma.

Q: What was the tunnel used for in the Unmentionable Times?

AR: It was a subway.

Q: Why did this society come to be, and how could it get so out of hand that almost everything was a transgression?

AR: The reason, [with respect to] both parts of the question, lies in the philosophy that men accepted (see my answer to the fifth question). When men have no rights, when they are expected to live for the sake of others, anything they do for their own sake would be regarded by their rulers as a transgression.

Q: Who picked the people for the World Council?

AR: The gang entrenched in the World Council would choose its own members and perpetuate itself. As an example of such politics, see the government of Soviet Russia.

Q: Why was unhappiness against the law?

AR: Because the rulers wanted no complaints; they wanted the slaves to pretend to be satisfied with the conditions of their existence.

Q: Why was 40-45 considered old?

AR: Because life was so hard in such a society that men were worn out and few were able to survive to the age of 45. It is an historical fact that in primitive, preindustrial societies, men's life-expectancy was 20 years. (It is 72 today.)

Q: How long did it take you to write *Anthem*?

AR: About three months.

Q: How did you get the idea for the theme?

AR: I got the idea in my school days, in Soviet Russia, when I heard all the vicious attacks on individualism, and asked myself what the world would be like if men lost the word "I."

Q: What kinds of religions existed in this society?

AR: The worship of the state, of the collective, was that society's religion.

Q: Why did you choose the title *Anthem*?

AR: Because this story is my hymn to man's ego.

Why I Like Stamp Collecting

This article originally appeared in the Minkus Stamp Journal *in 1971.*

I started collecting stamps when I was ten years old, but had to give it up by the time I was twelve. In all the years since, I never thought of resuming the hobby. It left only one after-effect: I was unable to throw away an interesting-looking stamp. So, I kept saving odd stamps, all these years; I put them into random envelopes and never looked at them again.

Then, about a year-and-a-half ago, I met a bright little girl named Tammy, who asked me—somewhat timidly, but very resolutely—whether I received letters from foreign countries and, if I did, would I give her the stamps. I promised to send her my duplicates. She was eleven years old, and so intensely serious about her collection that she reminded me of myself at that age.

Once I started sorting out the stamps I had accumulated, I was hooked.

It was an astonishing experience to find my enthusiasm returning after more than fifty years, as if there had been no interruption. Only now the feeling had the eagerness of childhood combined with the full awareness, confidence and freedom of age.

My first step was to acquire a Minkus Master Global Stamp Album. In a year and a half, it has grown to four volumes, plus four special albums—and my collection is still growing, at an accelerating rate. No, I have not forgotten Tammy: I send her piles of duplicates every few months, and I feel very grateful to her.

In all those years, I had never found a remedy for mental fatigue. Now, if I feel tired after a whole day of writing, I spend an hour with my stamp albums and it makes me able to resume writing for the rest of the evening. A stamp album is a miraculous brain-restorer.

I am often asked why people like stamp collecting. So widespread a hobby can obviously have many different motives. I can answer only in regard to my own motives, which I have observed also in some of the stamp collectors I have met.

The pleasure lies in a certain special way of using one's mind. Stamp collecting is a hobby for busy, purposeful, ambitious people—because, in pattern, it has the essential elements of a career, but transposed to a clearly delimited, intensely private world.

A career requires the ability to sustain a purpose over a long period of time, through many separate steps, choices, decisions, adding up to a steady progression toward a goal. Purposeful people cannot rest by doing nothing; nor can they feel at home in the role of passive spectators. They seldom find pleasure in single occasions, such as a party or a show or even a vacation, a pleasure that ends right then and there, with no further consequences.

The minds of such people require continuity, integration, a sense of moving forward. They are accustomed to working long-range; to them, the present is part of and a means to the future; a short-range event or activity that leads nowhere is an unnatural strain on them, an irritating interruption or a source of painful boredom.

Yet they need relaxation and rest from their constant, single-tracked drive. What they need is another track, but for the same train—that is, a change of subject, but using part of the same method of mental functioning.

Stamp collecting fulfills that need.

It establishes a wide context of its own, interesting enough to hold one's attention and to switch one's mind temporarily away from exhausting problems or burdens.

In the course of a career, every achievement is an end in itself and, simultaneously, a step toward further achievements. In collecting, every new stamp is an event, a pleasure in itself and, simultaneously, a step toward the growth of one's collection. A collector is not a passive spectator, but an active, purposeful agent in a cumulative drive. He cannot stand still: an album page without fresh additions becomes a reproach, an almost irresistible call to embark on a new quest.

In a career, there is no such thing as achieving too much: the more one does, the more one loves one's work. In collecting, there is no such thing as too many stamps: the more one gets, the more one wants. The sense of action, of movement, of progression is wonderful—and habit-forming.

There are also certain differences.

Stamp collecting is an adjunct of, not a substitute for, a career. A career requires problem-solving—creative problems, technical problems, business problems, etc. Stamp collecting requires a full, focused attention, but no problem-solving; it is a process of cashing in on the given and known. If one makes it a substitute for productive work, it becomes an empty escape; an unproductive mind does not need rest.

The course of a career depends on one's own action predominantly, but not exclusively. A career requires a struggle; it involves tension, disappointments, obstacles which are challenging, at times, but are often ugly, painful, senseless—particularly, in an age like the present, when one has to fight too frequently against the dishonesty, the evasions, the irrationality of the people one deals with. In stamp collecting, one experiences the rare pleasure of independent action without irrelevant burdens or impositions. Nobody can interfere with one's collection, nobody need be considered or questioned or worried about. The choices, the work, the responsibility—and the enjoyment—are one's own. So is the great sense of freedom and privacy.

For this very reason, when one deals with people as a stamp collector, it is on a cheerful, benevolent basis. People cannot interfere, but they can be very helpful and generous. There is a sense of "brotherhood" among stamp collectors, of a kind which is very unusual today: the brotherhood of holding the same values. In the midst of today's cynical inversion and corruption of all values, one seldom meets a person with whom one has any interest in common; most people today do not actually value or enjoy anything. Stamp collectors have a wide latitude of individual preferences, but the basic principles of the hobby are objective and clear-cut. A stamp collector would not reject the one-cent British Guiana on the grounds that it is unique—and he would not exchange it for a dozen German Inflation stamps on the grounds that these were more fashionable since more people used them.

The pursuit of the unique, the unusual, the different, the rare is the motive power of stamp collecting. It endows the hobby with the suspense and excitement of a treasure hunt—even on the more modest levels of collecting, where the treasure may be simply an unexpected gift from a friend, which fills the one blank spot, completing a set.

This mood of lighthearted benevolence is particularly important to people whose careers deal with grim, crucial issues—as, for instance, a writer who studies the trends of the modern world, or a surgeon who faces the constant question of life or death. It is not an accident that a great many doctors are stamp collectors.

Careers of that kind require such a ruthless discipline of total dedication that one can become almost depersonalized. This is why an hour spent on an activity whose sole purpose is one's own pleasure, becomes such a restoring, invigorating life line.

When one turns to stamps, one enters a special world by a process resembling a response to art: one deals with an isolated and stressed aspect of existence—and one experiences the sense of a clean, orderly, peaceful, sunlit world. Its rules and boundaries are strictly delimited—the rest is up to one's individual choice. But one does not choose blindly, one deals with firm, intelligible, changeless things. There is constant change in the world of stamps, and constant motion, and a brilliant flow of color, and a spectacular display of human imagination—but there is no change in the nature and purpose of stamps. Nobody tries to claim—as people do in other fields—that a wilted scrap of lettuce from his garbage can is a superior kind of stamp. It is not the place for whims, it is not a world for those who like the chaos of undefinable, shifting, whirling, drippy emotions. It is a world for orderly, rational minds.

But—it is asked—why not collect cigar bands, or coins, or old porcelain? Why stamps?

Because stamps are the concrete, visible symbols of an enormous abstraction: of the communications net embracing the world.

An inextricable part of even a casual glance at stamps is the awareness of what a magnificent achievement they represent: for a few pennies, you can send a letter to any place on earth, to the farthest, most desolate corner where human beings might live—to Greenland or to the Cocos (Keeling) Islands (population: 1000). Those bright little pieces of paper will carry your words across oceans, over mountains, over deserts, and still more difficult: over savage frontiers (the most savage of which are not on the underdeveloped continents). Stamps, as a postal institution, are only 130 years old. Think of the human ingenuity, the technological development, the large-scale synchronization of effort that were required to create a worldwide postal system. (You may curse the inefficiency of your local post offices—and the ones abroad may be worse—but look at the total picture of what they are accomplishing.)

While the world politicians are doing their best to split the globe apart by means of iron curtains and brute force, the world postal services are demonstrating—in their quiet, unobtrusive way—what is required to bring mankind closer together: a specific purpose cooperatively carried out, serving individual goals and needs. It is the voices of individual men that stamps carry around the globe; it is individual men that need a postal service; kings, dictators and other rulers do not work by mail. In this sense, stamps are the world's ambassadors of good will.

Stamp collecting gives one a large-scale view of the world—and a very benevolent view. One feels: no matter how dreadful some of mankind's activities might be, here is a field in which men are functioning reasonably, efficiently and successfully. (I do not mean the political set-up involved, I mean the technical aspects and skills required to deliver the world's gigantic tonnage of mail.)

When I hear in the news the name of some country that I discovered only through my stamp album—such as Tonga or Niue—I feel a touch of personal recognition, like an affectionate greeting. Stamps give one a personal value-stake, a kind of proprietary interest in distant lands which, otherwise, would remain mere names and empty abstractions. (Some countries are abusing this and putting out an unconscionable amount of philatelic waste, more stamps than could possibly be used for legitimate postal needs. But collectors are free to ignore them.) A stamp album is like a world tour, with the advantage of focusing selectively on the best aspects of various cultures, and without the bitter disadvantages.

Speaking esthetically, I should like to mention the enormous amount of talent displayed on stamps—more than one can find in today's art galleries. Ignoring the mug shots of some of the world's ugliest faces (a sin of which the stamps of most countries are guilty), one finds real little masterpieces of the art of painting. In this respect, the stamps of Japan are consistently the best. But my personal favorites are two smaller countries whose stamps are less well known: Ryukyu Islands and Iceland. If this were a competition, I would give first prize, for beauty of design, to two stamps of Iceland that feature stylized drawings of trees.

In conclusion, I want to say a personal "thank you" to a man whose extremely generous interest and guidance have helped me to find my way in a very complex field: Mr. Jacques Minkus. The infectiously irresistible enthusiasm he projects for the world of stamps, and the glamor of the philatelic establishment he has created give him an unusual position in today's cheerless world: the head of an empire dedicated to human enjoyment.

INDEX

A

September 23 — "Blind Chaos" — (The Algerian situation &
Kennedy's anti-ideology)
(Politics — foreign policy)

September 30 — "The Man-Haters" — (Altruism as a doctrine of hatred
for man. Examples: The Constitution —
The Civil War — today's policy toward the
"underdeveloped" nations.)
(Politics — ethics & foreign aid)

October 7 — "The Season of Platitudes" — (The generalities of election
campaigns)
(Politics — elections)

October 14 — "Our Alleged Competitor" — (The economic state of Sov.
Russia) (Politics — Russia)

October 21 — "Britain's 'National Socialism'" — (Gaitskell & Common
Market)(Politics — England)

October 28 — "Nationalism versus Internationalism" — (Internationalism &
Common Market)
(Politics — foreign affairs)

Nov. 4 — published above article

Nov. 11 — "The Cuban 'Crisis'" — (Kennedy & U.N.)
(Politics — Cuba)

Nov. 18 — "Post-Mortem, 1962" — (The election)
(Politics — domestic)

Nov. 25 – "How to Demoralize a Nation" – (Kennedy's visit to the
                                          Soviet Ballet – and the
                                          Cuban crisis)
                                          (Politics – foreign)

Dec. 2 – "Freedom of Speech" – (Hiss' TV appearance – Private rights vs.
                                gov. suppression) (Politics – theory)

Dec. 9 – "The Munich of World War III ?" (The Cuban crisis – & its aftermath
                                          in the U.N.) (Politics – foreign)

Dec. 16 – "Vandalism" (TV "Cyrano de Bergerac") (Art – culture)